A YEAR OF CREATIVITY

A YEAR OF CREATIVITY

a craft date planner

to meet, share, and create

Petra Hoeksema

Lidy Nooij

Miriam Catshoek

Bregje Konings

Brimming with creative inspiration, how-to projects, and useful information to enrich your everyday life, Quarto Knows is a favorite destination for those pursuing their interests and passions. Visit our site and dig deeper with our books into your area of interest: Quarto Creates, Quarto Cooks, Quarto Homes, Quarto Lives, Quarto Drives, Quarto Explores, Quarto Gifts, or Quarto Kids.

First Published in the USA in 2019 by Quarry Books, an imprint of The Quarto Group,
100 Cummings Center, Suite 265-D, Beverly, MA 01915, USA.
T (978) 282-9590 F (978) 283-2742 QuartoKnows.com

Quarry Books titles are also available at discount for retail, wholesale, promotional, and bulk purchase. For details, contact the Special Sales Manager by email at specialsales@quarto.com or by mail at The Quarto Group, Attn: Special Sales Manager, 100 Cummings Center, Suite 265-D, Beverly, MA 01915, USA.

10 9 8 7 6 5 4 3 2

ISBN: 978-1-63159-817-3

Digital edition published in 2019

Library of Congress Cataloging-in-Publication Data available

Concept, projects, patterns and styling:
Miriam Catshoek, Bregje Konings, Lidy Nooij, and Petra Hoeksema

Composition, design, cover and illustrations: Eline Pellinkhof

Layout: Antoinette van Schaik (Instagram: wat_maakt_ze_nu_weer)

Photography cover and projects:
Anna Visser – Laif Fotographie (Instagram: laiffotographie)

Photography PACKAGIN INSPIRATION:
Lidy, Petra, Bregje, Miriam and Eline

Translation: Jessica Kroezen

Printed in China

I RIP STITCHES
YOU RIP STITCHES
WE RIPPED STITCHES

CONTENTS

short projects

longer projects

weekend or cooperative projects

DO
SOMETHING
creative
EVERY
DAY

INTRODUCTION

A brand-new concept that has emerged in the world of crafting and hobbies is the "Craft Date." Here is a brief description. The concept is described in more detail later in the book.

A Craft Date is a fun date with a handful of creative-types in which you surprise each other with craft and DIY projects and specific materials and make beautiful things together.

At each date, a group of participants come up with a self-made project to be carried out by the other attendees and provide everyone with the necessary materials. These materials are chosen based on the specific taste of each attendee and are packaged up and given like a unique personal gift. With these gifts and the step-by-step instructions of the planners in hand, everyone gets to work.

A Craft Date is different than a workshop since you get to choose the lovely people that you want to invite. And as organizer, you get to participate in all the projects and are also surprised by the others. All of the invitees can put their own spin on the project by using their favorite colors, materials, or techniques. This way, you end up with lots of different interpretations and results, leading to new inspiration and ideas.

FOREWORD

Craft Dates. Crafting together, but with your own style and colors. Surprising each other with creative assignments, projects, and beautiful materials. Chatting with the others, enjoying something tasty, and inspiring each other.

The idea of organizing or participating in a Craft Date was, initially, completely new to me. But for the four friends, Petra Hoeksema, Lidy Nooij, Miriam Catshoek, and Bregje Konings, it has been their go-to way of making time for each other and for doing what they love to do, namely, crafting, since forever.

I don't actually know how well-known the term crafting has become. In the world of Bregje, Miriam, Lidy, and Petra, it's so ingrained that I find myself using it to describe anything from handiwork to do-it-yourself projects. And crafting can involve virtually any material or technique you can imagine. From one moment to the next, the ladies might be crocheting or painting (wearing a self-made apron) or twisting a screw into a piece of wood . . . .

The idea to create a book about crafting came up about a year ago when Petra, full of enthusiasm, told me all about their famous creative get-togethers at lunch one day. "You write a book about this!" It needed to be a book that not only provided instructions on how to organize your own Craft Date, but also included examples of projects that you might do during a date. It needed to provide clear instructions and examples to inspire creative ways of packaging up the materials.

ONE BOOK, FOUR AUTHORS
BECAUSE A CRAFT DATE IS SOMETHING YOU DO TOGETHER
AND CREATING A BOOK ABOUT IT IS, TOO

The added value of a book written by four authors is that every author adds her own "'handwriting." This is how many of the projects in this book ended up being completed in four different styles and four different color combinations and is why it is even more inspiring and puts forward even more ideas. And even though each of the four has a different style, they complement each other perfectly. What the four have in common is their eye for detail, their nose for quality when it comes to materials and tools, and their perfectionism when it comes to technique and workmanship.

Before we started the book, we created a color pallet of all of the favorite colors of the members of the team. With the pallet in hand, we chose all of the yarns, fabrics, and other materials, which formed a lovely, coherent whole.

And hours and hours were spent knitting, crocheting, embroidering, sewing, painting, working with paper, and sometimes even baking—by all four. Many projects were conceived of, from simple ones that can be completed in about an hour, to elaborate ones that might take a whole day or even a weekend to complete. Craft Dates were even organized especially for the book, where piles and piles of photos were taken, some of which you'll find in this book.

And while the ladies were extremely busy crafting and organizing, there I was, behind the scenes, working on the planning and the design of the concept. And, of course, I also took part in my very first Craft Date so that I could be part of the conversation and know, firsthand, how inspiring they can be. It makes you want to organize your very own! Really!

A BOOK FULL OF INSPIRATION

It is a book for everyone with a basic knowledge of crocheting, knitting, and sewing. We are not going to teach you how to crochet or explain how a sewing machine works. There are plenty of other books for that and many videos on the Internet. What we do do is try to make everyone enthusiastic about getting together and crafting because it's so much better doing it together than alone. It's more fun, helps you get going on projects, and the exchange of ideas and tips makes it so inspiring. You discover new magazines, books, or new craft stores and visit each other's "craft rooms," and it is a way of guaranteeing that you free up a bit of time for yourself.

COMMUNITY

Have you had a great Craft Date or are you working on a neat project and want to show it off? There's a place for this in the Craft Dates Community. On Instagram, for example, you can tag your photos with, or search for, **#craftdates**. You can have a look at each other's work, drum up inspiration for your own dates, invite your Insta-friends, or organize a "blind date" with creative people from your town or city that you don't yet know.

A whole world will open up—a very creative world. And I'm proud to say that I was a part of it at the very beginning, together with my four incredibly sweet and creative friends.

Eline Pellinkhof
Author *Eline's Huis*
Instagram: *elinepellinkhof*

The Craft Dates color card

THE AUTHORS

From left to right: Petra, Miriam, Lidy, and Bregje

ABOUT BREGJE
Instagram: bregjekonings
Blog: needlesbybregje.blogspot.nl

I've been crafting and fiddling around with cloth, thread, paper, and paint for as long as I can remember. I suppose it is somewhat unsurprising being the daughter of two artists and one of four sisters, all of whom made a career out of their creative talents. My passion is working with textiles. I got my first Singer sewing machine when I was eight years old.

While my friends were outside roller skating, I was wandering through old craft markets and doll museums. Even then I had an interest in pure materials, traditional techniques, and classic detail. I also always wanted to know exactly how things were made—what they were made of, which tools were used to make them, and, most of all, why they were made. I spent hours behind the sewing machine, trying everything out. I loved it, especially at night when the world consisted only of my hands and my work.

It went almost without saying that I ended up in education, specifically in a program to train teachers in the area of Drawing and Textile Methods. I graduated with a specialization in Fashion and Clothing. I wanted to share my passion for textile with others.

Because the teaching and sharing of knowledge with others is as much fun as time spent sewing your own clothes, crocheting scarves, knitting cardigans, dying wool, and spinning yarn. I get to do this every day in my wonderful home studio, where the door is always open. Friends and students come by often

for a knitting/crocheting/spinning lesson or just for coffee and a chat. The cabinets are literally erupting with swatches of fabric, balls of wool, rolls of ribbon, cards wound with lace, boxes of buttons, and pots of paint. There are sewing machines, sergers, spinning wheels, and looms. There's no shortage of materials or inspiration.

I prefer to make things that are reversible and can be worn inside out, and yes, I like to make things difficult for myself. Whatever isn't good enough gets taken apart. "Twice as much fun for the price of one" as I like to say.

There are no stark contrasts and hard lines for me. I strive for subtlety in color, detail, and finishing. As precise as I am in my work, the area around me tends to end up a mess. My studio looks like it exploded and, afterward, everything is "neatly" stuffed into the cabinets again, just in time for the next sewing lesson, workshop, knitting club, or spinning group.

And surprise, surprise! I tend to "temporarily" misplace things. Thankfully, this doesn't tend to last long because I almost never throw anything away. You can always use it make something! I'M NOT MESSY; I'M CREATIVELY ORGANIZED.

ABOUT MIRIAM
Instagram: miriamcatshoek

It's funny, I've never really seen myself as a creative person.

There were always people around me who, I felt, were so much more creative. There was my mother, who was always behind the sewing machine or knitting or crocheting and who would craft with us endlessly. There was my sister, Lidy, who can do just about anything—what her eyes see, her hands make.

My studio (Bregje)

Fashion, that was something I liked. I started to sew my own pants (in my house, you got your own sewing machine on your sixteenth birthday), knit simple sweaters, and alter clothes. I drew inspiration from the piles of magazines I bought. I still have a weakness for beautiful magazines—ones about fashion, interior design, and styling. These days, I enjoy working with paper, stamps, and punches to make cards, cool labels, and packaging. I love packing things up and wrapping things. I make a real project out of it.

The sewing machine has also stuck around. At sewing lessons with a true, old-fashioned dressmaker, reviewing everything from bound buttonholes to a clothesline in the seam of collars . . . I learned a lot, but I still find it difficult to sew in a zipper! I used to make a fair amount of clothing for my two daughters. It's great picking out beautiful fabrics and then getting to work with them.

And then came crocheting and the love of wool that accompanied it—blankets, scarves, and rustic-looking poufs for the home. Basic and robust—that really sums up my style. There's nothing fiddly, no complicated patterns, just beautiful yarn, in a simple pattern, in my favorite colors: lots of grey, old rose, and grey-green. Combining colors is something I enjoy—creating a lovely "bouquet" of balls of yarn in your arms and then having a look, choosing combinations and matching.

There are so many beautiful things on Instagram these days. Instagram has changed the way I look at things. I do my best to take good photos: styling

and shuffling things around for that one perfect shot. It's where I discovered that there are others out there who are made happy by a ball of wool and a nice vase and that people were organizing very hip knitting parties where you could meet all those other knitting and wool enthusiasts in person. What is better than being able to share your passion with others, chatting endlessly about beautiful yarns, the best crochet hooks, the nicest patterns, all the while with your telephone sitting there on the table. Because at these parties, no one looks at you funny if you stand up on your chair so that you can take the best possible picture of the table from above or if you adjust the position of a pair of scissors three times to get the shot you want. I've crossed paths with so many great people and taken on so many new, inspiring challenges, all because of Instagram.

With my full-time job as dental assistant and my family, things are always busy. That's why I love spending time at home, making the house and garden welcoming by adding some styling here and there and a vase of fresh flowers on the table and switching on Netflix! My "collection" of project bags is located next to the couch—I usually have around four projects on the go. Happily knitting my stress away is how I relax. Finishing something off before starting a new project? I don't subscribe to that. There's always a new idea rolling around in my head. And how great is it that I get to share all of this with my sister and good friends? Crafting together, inspiring each other, and helping.

ABOUT LIDY
Instagram: lidynooij
Blog: lidynooij.com

Craftiness is happiness. Crafting is a lifestyle to me.

I've been creating for my entire life. When I was twelve, I got my first sewing machine and started sewing clothes for my dolls, decorated jars with embroidered bits of felt, and made perfume from rose petals. At school, I was already organizing crafting afternoons with friends for other kids. Creativity was always present at home. My mother would sit behind the sewing machine or knit every single day.

I don't like to pin myself down to one technique. There is so much out there in terms of beautiful and interesting handiwork, and I want to try everything. I want to be able to do everything and so I'm always learning.

My style (Miriam)

My studio (Lidy)

Every day, you'll find me in my studio or on the couch working on a knitting or crocheting project. My studio takes up about half of the upstairs of my house, but, to be honest, my entire house is a creative studio! I keep and collect just about anything that might be useful at some point in the future. I like to scour rummage sales and thrift shops.

Over the years, I've participated in a variety of workshops on things ranging from crocheting and tanning, to lace making and painting, and from quilting to dressmaking. But for the most part, I'm self-taught, just learning by doing and discovering. I usually have some kind of finished product in mind, but it's the getting there that I find so interesting and fun. Sometimes, I enjoy the process most of all. Combining difference (old handiwork) techniques and materials in one project is one of my favorite challenges. And, of course, I have an eye for detail and finishing. I have also held many different workshops. I've also organized "crocheting teas:" crocheting parties with tasty treats on the side.

These days, social media is the way to connect to other creative types. There's a real sense of recognition when you discover, on Instagram, for example, that there are other people out there that are as into beautiful colors and cool materials as you are. I've established a whole collection of craft friends this way.

For the past few years, I've also been a member of the Craft Kitchen team. Together with other Craft Kitchen ladies, I attend conferences and write a blog (www.craftkitchen.nl). Crafting, creating, chatting, and networking with fun, enthusiastic people who all share an interest or passion is what I love to do. This is why this Craft Dates book just needed to be written.

ABOUT PETRA
Instagram: bypetra

I've been doing handiwork since elementary school. When I turned four, my grandmother gave me a toy sewing machine and my first project was a dress for my sister, which she even wore. Later, I remember taking out every single issue of the magazine Ariadne from the library (back when it really was just a handiwork magazine) and teaching myself to embroider and crochet. With the help of Knip Mode magazine and my great grandmother's old sewing machine, I learned how to sew clothes. Later, my aunt gave me a very solid Vendex sewing machine that I used for years.

During my studies at university (technical business administration and physics) and in the first couple of years of work (as an IT specialist at IBM), I didn't do any handiwork at all. But when I entered a study program in graphic design, I really enjoyed being able to work with color and color combinations. It was only when I found myself on the verge of a burnout that I started doing handiwork again, and I haven't stopped since.

I started up a blog to get in touch with other creative types. In 2010, I created an online store that sold creative materials, and I had the opportunity to work on the Eline's Huis books. During a sabbatical, I worked on two of my own books and appeared in several magazines—including Mollie Makes! I was

My favorite colors and my cat Roosje (Petra)

also active on my own blog on which I shared lots of project ideas, but these days, you'll find me almost entirely on Instagram.

Four years ago, I took on a new role at IBM that requires me to travel a fair amount, I was no longer able to combine my online store with my work. When I closed the online store, I felt a sense of freedom to be able to work on my own creative projects again and to just be a consumer again. All of a sudden, I had time to seek out beautiful materials and tools and to try out new techniques.

In the meantime, I've learned to felt, weave, crochet, knit, sew, work with wood, graphic design, doll making . . . Am I forgetting anything? Probably! As of a couple of years ago, I started making Waldorf-style dolls for whom I love designing and making clothes—knitted and crocheted, of course, but also just sewn on the sewing machine.

I'm a creative jack-of-all-trades, who's also very handy with computers. How often do I get asked if I made something myself? The people around me are convinced I can do just about anything. I love a variety of techniques, but I find myself knitting and crocheting the most. Those are also the projects that are the easiest to take along with me when I have to travel for work or when go on vacation. I'm also crazy about modern, Japanese handiwork books, tools, and materials. And I try to convey the style in this book.

HOW IT ALL BEGAN

Six years ago, I (Petra) met Lidy, Miriam, and Bregje for the first time at a Handiwork convention in Zwolle. I was there for my Petra store and Miriam had added my stand to her "to-see" list because I sold Eline's Huis materials. We all got to talking and discovered that we lived nearby each other. One thing led to another, and we made a date to meet in my studio in Amsterdam. It was the second day of the Pentecost, a super warm, summery day, but we stayed inside to craft. We agreed in advance that we would each bring with us a project to be made with materials for everyone. We hadn't planned it, but all of us ended up packaging up the materials in lovely wrapping so that everyone got to open a special gift every time. It was such fun!

We found this so inspiring that we started doing it more often. Sometimes, we would work on the same project, but each of us would give it our own spin. We even went away for a weekend together for which we thought up the perfect project to do during our time away.

It has become a tradition to organize a surprise Craft Date for a fiftieth birthday. Of course, it also includes lunch, treats, and perfect styling! (Unfortunately for me, it'll be a while before I turn fifty. . .)

Petra

HOW DOES A CRAFT DATE WORK?

Our Craft Dates started off being spontaneous and coincidental, as you have just read. Now, we've developed them into a concept that can take on a variety of forms.

PACKAGING OF MATERIALS
What every date has in common is that we package up everything beautifully for each other. The basic supplies are compiled and the haberdashery—how great is that word?—is sourced. All the materials are as color coordinated as possible. It makes us happy, time and time again: from the way materials are packaged, to swatches of fabric, labels, stamps, and sometimes even the scissors on the table. Yes, we even like to make sure the pin heads and the stitch markers are in color! Everything is carefully placed in self-sewn or self-stuck packaging and sealed with string, tape, or a lovely clip and, of course, a self-made (name) tag is added as a finishing touch. This way, when everyone arrives, a personal gift awaits them, which is unpacked and used to carry out the project. Just this part alone makes a date festive!

And if you find yourself thinking, "oh man, what a ton of work!"—don't. It's precisely the looking in advance for lovely details for the project, the packaging, or even just giving a gift to your friends that makes the lead up to a Craft Date so much fun. Along the way, you'll come up with more and more ideas. And for those of you who are less inclined on the wrapping front, this book will be of help as we include a great deal of packaging inspiration throughout.

DIFFERENT KINDS OF CRAFT DATES

There are a number of different types of Craft Dates that we tend to hold, but there are probably countless other ways you might think of to organize a Craft Date. Below are our Craft Date themes:

CRAFT DATE WITH SEVERAL QUICK PROJECTS
This was our first Craft Date: a day-long date in which all four of us come up with and prepared small projects for each other. They are small in scale so that we can finish all four of them in the time we have. Day-long means that we also provide everyone with tasty bites and lunch in between.

CRAFT DATE WITH ONE PROJECT PER PERSON
We also have dates where we all work on one project individually. This might be a project that takes longer to complete and that you can take home and finish there. Examples of projects include sewing a dress or apron or crocheting a bag or scarf. It's so great to share our knowledge and inspiration with each other this way.

COOPERATIVE CRAFT DATE
During this kind of date, we all work together on one project, like a beautiful present for a mutual friend. Each of us might crochet a pile of granny squares in her own style that are put together to form an amazing blanket or a nice set of cushions, each one with a different crochet or knitting stitch. This type of date is a great one for baby showers or bachelorette parties.

SURPRISE CRAFT DATE
Another fun option is the surprise date. It involves surprising one of the Craft Date ladies, often around her birthday, kidnapping her, and taking her away for a Craft Date "on the road." The whole day is planned out: visiting stores, museums or workshops, the drinks, and the picnic. The kidnapped Craft Date participant is along for the ride and just has to sit back and enjoy!

WEEKEND CRAFT DATE

This is the deluxe version of a Craft Date that lasts an entire weekend. It's an escape from busy home lives, work, and getting up early. It's about enjoying a weekend full of anything and everything to do with crafting. Our wonderful weekend date was on the island of Texel, in a cozy little house with bags full of wool, more than we could ever use up, of course, tasty treats, and our own crochet blankets for curling up on the couch; visiting crafty shops and coming up with ideas in the village; and of course, we also enjoyed a walk on the beach and the cup of hot chocolate afterward at the beach café. We did draw a bit of attention there for sitting around the woodstove, crocheting. Our homemade project bags go everywhere with us because:

Bregje

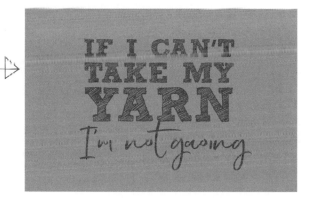

AND THEN . . .

Inviting

I always enjoy a Craft Date. Not only the date itself, but also the fun in advance, making all the necessary preparations is great. It all starts with making a Craft Date.

You can, of course, always have dates with creative types that you know, but, in using platforms like Instagram, I've gotten to know creative people across the whole country. It's so great to meet these people in real life and craft with them. So, don't hesitate to just invite some of those fun people over to your home. It can lead to beautiful new friendships.

You can always email your invitation to your guests. It's certainly handy given that we are all so busy these days and it's an easy way to settle on a date (a good website for this is datumprikker.nl) and discuss with the group. But it's more creative and personal to send out a self-made invitation in the mail. And who doesn't like receiving mail?

If you are planning to do more than one project in a day, do this with a small group of about four people. And make sure you agree beforehand that these projects will take no more than two hours apiece. The projects shouldn't be all that complicated, so think of fun, small-scale, do-it-yourself projects. Everything doesn't always have to be completely finished at the end of the day, but it is nice to be able to show each other the finished products at the end of the day and to take pictures.

You can always plan a follow-up date.

THINKING UP PROJECTS

This book is, of course, filled with inspiration for projects, and there are other books and magazines out there. Instagram and especially Pinterest are filled with great creations, patterns, and ideas. You don't need to think everything up yourself. Let yourself be inspired and give an existing project your own twist.

You can choose to make an example of the project you came up with so that you can show it to the others at the beginning of the date. This can be helpful because everyone can see exactly what you have in mind. But it's not necessary. Simply getting to work together on a new idea is just as good. If patterns are required, or written instructions, make them on the computer and print them out for everyone. Pack them up alongside the materials.

CHOOSING MATERIALS FOR EACH OTHER

Once you've thought of a fun project and invited your participants, you can start thinking about which materials you'd like to buy or put together for each person. If you know someone well, then you'll probably already know what his or her style is—rustic, romantic, hip, colorful or very pastel colors or only neutrals. Think about the style of the homes of your participants, which colors they tend toward. If you don't know the person well, check and see if they have an Instagram account and have a look there. If it's still not entirely clear, just ask your participants what their preference is because it's so much fun to make everything more personal.

INDIVIDUAL STYLE

During our dates, it is always the case that while we all start out with the same project, we end up with quite different, personal finished products. The differences can come from the different colors or materials used, or the scale of the project, or the placement of labels, etc. Everyone gets the chances to put their own spin on things, making them unique and representative of everyone's individual style. So, just be yourself when you're crafting together. There are no rules. And if you aren't sure what direction to go in, let yourself be inspired by the others.

Lidy

PROJECTS

MIRIAM'S CROCHET GLASS VASES

handmade
WITH LOVE

You can never have too many containers . . . I love them! I collected a whole bunch of square, glass vases at the thrift store. You can find them there in all sorts of sizes. Use chunky wool or rustic jute to crochet a sleeve for the container, a fun and simple project. Give everyone a plant to go in it and you're all set. I personally love doing this kind of project and really enjoy giving the finished project as a gift.

What follows is a pattern for a fairly tall container. For shorter containers, adjust the pattern yourself accordingly. Use a combination of the rows described below until you achieve the desired height.

Crochet a row of chain stitches and finish with a slip stitch. Measure your vase to see how long the circle needs to be. Be sure not to make it too loose!

Close every row with a slip stitch.

Row 1: Make 1 chain stitch and make 1 single crochet in every chain stitch.
Row 2: Make 2 chain stitches and make 1 half double crochet in every stitch.
Row 3: Make 1 chain stitch and make 1 single crochet in every stitch in the back loop.
Row 4: Repeat the row above.
Row 5: Make 2 chain stitches and make 1 half double crochet in every stitch.
Row 6: Repeat the row above.
Row 7: Make 3 chain stitches and make 1 double crochet in every stitch.
Row 8: Make 2 chain stitches and make 1 half double crochet in every stitch.
Row 9: Make 1 chain stitch and make 1 single crochet in every stitch in the back loop.
Row 10: Make 1 chain stitch and make 1 slip stitch in every stich.

Secure the loose yarn and slip the crochet sleeve on to the vase.

SUPPLIES
Square vase
Borgo de'Pazzi Bulky (about 3.5 ounces [100 g] for a large square vase)
Hoooked Natural Jute (optional)
Crochet hook N/P-15 (10 mm)
Darning needle

Green version is from Natural Jute (Hoooked)

SUPPLIES FOR LABEL
Sturdy Kraft paper/cardboard
Craft Dates die cutting template or
  pinking shears
Craft Dates stamp and stamp ink
Fabric hole punch
Robust yarn or thin string

LABEL
To finish off your project perfectly, add a sewn-on label to your crochet sleeve. Punch (Craft Date die cutting template COL1445) a label out of sturdy cardstock or cut out a 2.25 x 1.75 inch (5.5 x 4.5 cm) label using pinking shears. Stamp a cute image or text on to the label.

Punch holes on the sides using the hole punch and fasten your label to the sleeve with string or strong cotton yarn. Your container is now ready for use. Fill it with a cool plant, a nice bouquet of flowers, or your collection of crochet hooks.

Enjoy your hip, Craft Dates crochet vase!

PACKAGING INSPIRATION

Put all of the balls of Bulky yarn and some Natural Jute, if you are using it, in a large basket and place it in the middle of the table.

Set out the glass vases across the table and place a paper bag, decorated with patterned paper, stamps, and punched out figures, next to each vase.

These bags shown contain the (succulent) plants and a few prepunched labels that can be sewn on to the crochet sleeve later.

BREGJE'S PATTERN WEIGHTS

THEY KEEP YOUR DRAWING PAPER IN PLACE
WHEN YOU'RE TRACING A PATTERN

SUPPLIES

Scraps of cotton or linen fabric

Scissors

Craft Dates stamps or rubber stamps

Waterproof stamp ink (StazOn)

Aquarium gravel for the filling, preferably *not* sand

Pins

Needle and thread

Handle WITH ♡

Pattern weights are little bags filled with a weighted filling. They keep the pattern drawing paper nicely in its place when you're tracing a pattern from the original. Place a few here and there on your drawing paper so that it will stay put when you're tracing. They are super handy to have!

Cut the fabric scraps into 2.75 x 4.75 inch (7 x 12 cm) rectangles. This includes a 0.5 inch (1 cm) seam.

Stamp a small motif exactly in the middle of the square. It can be landscape or portrait orientation; it does not matter. Let the stamp dry.

Fold the rectangle, good-side facing inward, into a 2.5 x 2.75 inch (6 x 7 cm) square. Sew the side opposite to the fold closed. Sew one of the sides closed as well. You now have a small bag. Turn the bag.

Fold the open side over to create a 0.5 inch (1 cm) seam inward and smooth it out using your nail. This makes it a bit easier to pin it shut after you have filled it.

Fill the bag with a bit of gravel, just short of full. You'll need to twist it to sew the last seam closed to give the bag its pyramid shape.

Fold the open seam shut in such a way that it is perpendicular to the bottom—not parallel to the bottom, which will create a straight bag, not a pyramid. The pinned side seam is now in the middle on the back of the weight.

Pin the top with the previously folded 0.5 inch (1 cm) seam shut and sew the upper edge with small stiches, by hand, to close it.

Use this method to make as many weights as you'd like. Six of them will do a good job of holding a pattern in its place while cutting it out.

PACKAGING INSPIRATION

SUPPLIES

Kraft paper take-out containers (packaging materials)

Double-sided tape

Small plastic bags

Craft Dates die cutting template

Cardstock

Craft Dates stamp and stamp ink

Twine or kitchen string

White acrylic paint or chalk markers

Sticker

Black labels

Wax stamp, sealing wax

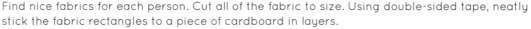

Find nice fabrics for each person. Cut all of the fabric to size. Using double-sided tape, neatly stick the fabric rectangles to a piece of cardboard in layers.

Fill small plastic bags with the gravel filling.

Punch or cut out a piece of cardstock to use as a needle book, fold in in half, and affix a piece of fabric, or not, to the inside in which to stick needles and pins (see page 39). Stamp a sewing machine or some other appropriate image on it.

Punch a small card on which to wrap thread in colors that match the fabrics. Put all of these items, along with the printed-out instructions in an envelope, in the take-out container. Wrap the container in twine and hang a small label on the twine with a sticker on which you write the name of the recipient. Write a lovely quote on the black label using white chalk marker and hang this on the box as well.

Finally, heat a small amount of the black sealing wax until it is fluid and pour this on to the closure on the lid of the box. Stamp the melted sealing wax with a nice wax stamp.

DO
SOMETHING
creative
EVERY
DAY

THIS IS HOW WE CROCHET A BLANKET

AFFORDABLE GRANNY BLANKETS
BY FOUR LADIES

Of course, it's always nice to work with beautiful, natural yarn—it's what we prefer—but when you want to make a bigger project, it can end up being very expensive. Thankfully, these days, there are a variety of acrylic yarns available that are machine washable and still feel soft. Bravo from Schachenmayr is an example of this kind of yarn that we like to work with, and it's available in an array of lovely colors. For this blanket, we each designed our own granny square. These squares can also be used for other projects.

SUPPLIES
Bravo, 4 different colors, 5 balls of each
Bravo, 1 joining color, 8 balls
Crochet hook 7 (4.5 mm)

COLOR NUMBERS
Pink 08305
Mint blue 08366
Green 08321
Salmon 08342
Grey 08295

The instructions for making the four different granny squares and for putting the blanket together can be found on pages 128–131.

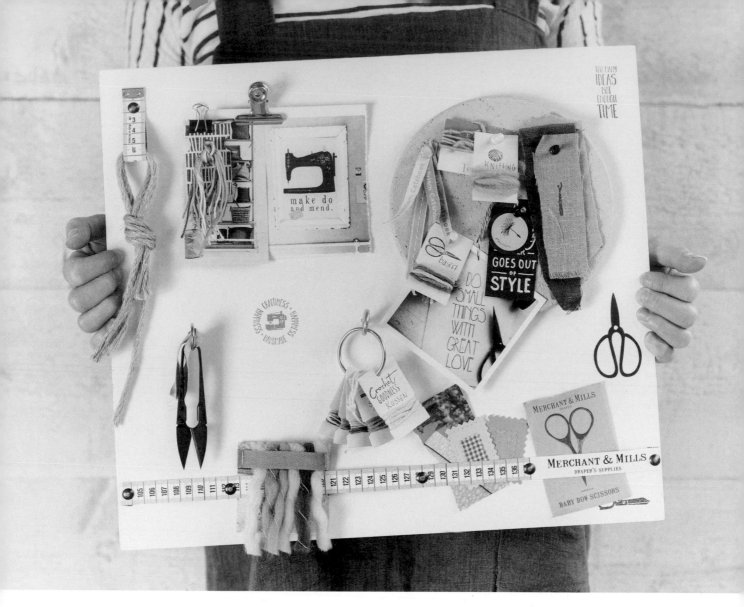

MIRIAM'S INSPIRATION BOARD

Paint the wooden board, as well as the cork coaster, using matte paint, in different colors, if you'd like. Decide on what you want to include on your inspiration board and organize it in a way that makes sense to you.

It's easiest to affix the coaster first by gluing it to the board. Cut your measuring tape to size and attach it to the board with tacks. Measure the things you want to insert behind the measuring tape (cards or pictures, for example) so that you can space out the tacks accordingly. Make a loop using the remaining measuring tape and attach the loop to the board with a tack. You can use the loop to hang yarn samples, among other things. Have a good look again at where you want to hang every-thing and attach the binder clip, hook, and screw eye/metal ring in the corresponding places.

A small screw should fit exactly through the hole in the binder clip. Use the bradawl to make a hole in the wood and screw the binder clips to the board.

Lidy

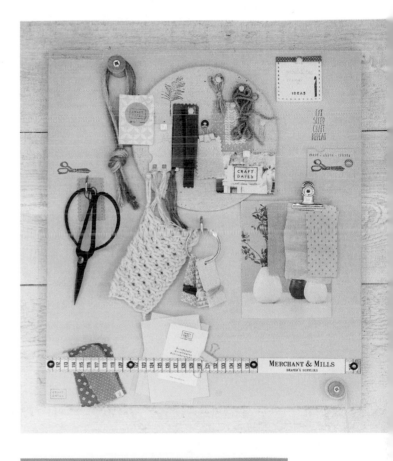

SUPPLIES

1 wooden board, 15.75 x 17.75 inches
 (40 x 45 cm)

Bradawl

Large cork placemat (from IKEA or
 Albert Heijn)

Matte paint (Dekor Paint Soft from Pentart),
 paint brush

Good glue (HT2 Gütermann Creativ)

Nice measuring tape to cut to size

Screw-in hook, screw eye, tacks, screws

Metal ring, binder clip

Nice scissors

Screwdriver, hammer

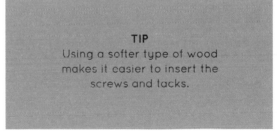

TIP
Using a softer type of wood
makes it easier to insert the
screws and tacks.

Now the "styling" of your board can begin. Pin cards that you like and pictures, etc. to your board. Hang your nicest scissors on the hook and make paper labels around which to wrap your favorite color combinations of yarns. You can hang these labels on the metal ring. It's always handy to be able to bring your best colors with you to stores or to Craft Dates.

Hang up your inspiration board in a good place in your craft room, hobby room, or studio or prop it up on a shelf where you can enjoy it fully!

Petra

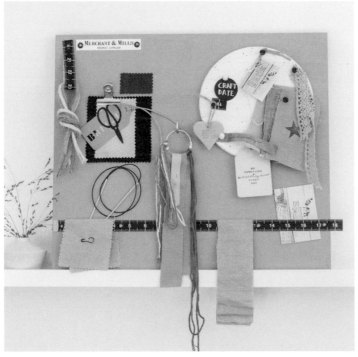

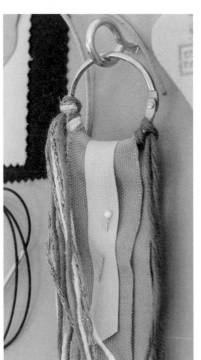

Bregje

PACKAGING INSPIRATION

Cover the table with a nice-looking vinyl table covering and place the wooden boards on top. On each board, place a nice, transparent, bag with a small piece of pretty wallpaper inside with "Craft Date" stamped on to it. Place all of the materials you'll need into this bag. In the middle of the table, place a rustic crate that contains all of the paints and brushes. Everyone should also get a small glass pot for a bit of water.

FOUR "ITALIAN" SCARVES

LINEN WITH A CROCHET EDGE

These "Italian" scarves get their name from the Italian origin of the linens used and the yarn.

Crochet
GOODNESS

All the instructions for making these beautiful scarves can be found on pages 137–139.

LIDY'S CANADIAN APPLE PIE

A Craft Date isn't complete without treats. Chatting, crafting, and treats! That's the foundation of any successful Craft Date. But many creative-types don't like spending too long in the kitchen. This apple pie is delicious and is super easy and quick to make. I'm a big fan!

TIP

If you have a Craft Date planned for a big group of people, just double this recipe and make the pie in a sheet pan, spreading the dough out across the entire pan.

INGREDIENTS (serves about 8)

4 apples

14 tablespoons (1¾ sticks, or 200 g) butter

2¼ cups (250 g) self-rising cake flour

1¼ cups (100 g) oatmeal

1 cup (225 g) brown sugar

Nuts (optional)

EQUIPMENT

8 x 2" (20 x 5 cm) springform pan

Parchment paper

DIRECTIONS

Wash the apples well.

Finely chop the apples, leaving the skin on.

Melt the butter in a small saucepan or in the microwave (do not overheat it).

Combine the self-rising flour, oatmeal, and brown sugar fully in a large bowl. Add the melted butter and stir well.

Preheat the oven to 350°F (180°C, or gas mark 4).

Line the springform pan with parchment paper.
Spread ¾ of the dough across the bottom of the pan and the sides, pressing it down firmly. Top the dough with the apple pieces, sprinkle the apple with a bit of cinnamon, and crumble the remaining dough over the top.

Bake the apple pie in a preheated oven for about an hour.

Bon appétit!

MIRIAM'S TOOL STATIONS
PRETTY AND USEFUL ADDITIONS TO YOUR CRAFT DATES TABLE

Here's a handy and fun tool station for the table during a Craft Date or even handier for your own craft table! I prefer not to have a bunch of loose items lying around on my work surface. If you're working on something creative with a group of people, your table will end up covered in materials and tools pretty quickly. That's what makes this handy tool station so great—it keeps all your tools in one place and looks great next to a vase of fresh flowers.

METHOD
Paint your tray in a color of your choosing and allow it to dry fully. Crochet a sleeve for the large jar (using the pattern for the square glass vases, for example).

Stick a piece of Aslan self-adhesive film to the back of your paper. Punch or cut out a nice label from your paper.

Add a nice stamp to your label or write something on it. Carefully remove the backing on the Aslan self-adhesive film and stick the label on your (fully degreased) small glass jar.

This is how you make the pincushion: fold your fabric in half with the reverse sides together and sew three sides. Leave one side open a bit so that you can turn it right-side out. You can also stitch in a label or a ribbon loop there. Turn your pincushion right-side out, stuff it with filling, and sew the opening closed by hand. Stick a few colorful pins into it and you're done!

Place crochet hooks, scissors, or markers in the large, crochet jar and place stitch markers, stitch rippers, threads, or flowers in the small one.

There are so many options and makes such a great gift to give!

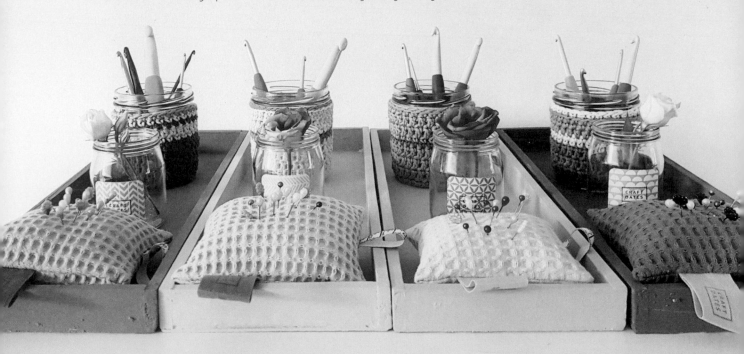

SUPPLIES

A simple, wooden candle tray or
  small serving tray

Matte paint, Dekor Paint Soft from
  Pentart, for example, and paintbrush

Empty, clean, glass (jam) jars

Cotton crochet yarn, Durable Double Four

Crochet hook

Darning needle

Aslan self-adhesive film (to make stickers)

Nice paper

Craft Date stamps and stamp ink

Fabric, about 6 x 11.75 inches (15 x 30 cm)

Sewing thread and a sewing machine

Ribbon for labels

Filling for pincushion

Pins

TIP
Matching the colors of all the
elements of your tool station yields the
best result. Try to pick paint,
fabric, paper, and yarn colors
that are complementary.

LIDY'S HABERDASHERY BAG
AND NEEDLE BOOK

**SUPPLIES FOR THE
HABERDASHERY BAG**
Unbleached cotton,
    2 pieces, 7.5 x 6 inches
    (19 x 15 cm) each
Craft Date stamps and-
    stamp ink
Piece of twill tape or
    ribbon
Pins
Needle and thread or
    sewing machine
Iron
Binder clip
Craft Dates paper
Craft Date die cutting
    templates
Notebook
Pencil

This is a great option for neatly packaging up all the notions and items (the haberdashery) you'll need for a Craft Date.

Make a bag from two pieces (7.5 x 6 inches [19 x 15 cm]) of unbleached cotton. Stamp and fold a piece of twill tape or ribbon and pin this between the two pieces of fabric as a label.

Sew the two pieces together on three sides, trim the corners, and turn the bag right-side out. Iron the bag flat and leave the opening unfinished.

Stamp the word haberdashery (using the Craft Dates stamp) on to the bag.

Fill the bag with whatever notions you'll need (for example, a tape measure with a stamped round sticker stuck on to it, a self-made needle book, and stitch markers).

Fold the top of the bag over to close, hold the fold in place with a binder clip, and tuck a few labels (made with Craft Dates paper and a Craft Dates die cutting template) under the clip, as well.

Buy a notebook and pencil and stamp some appropriate text on to in.

This makes a nice, stylish set to house supplies and it is a real gift for your guests.

SUPPLIES FOR THE NEEDLE BOOK
Sturdy (Craft Dates) paper
Craft Date Stamps and stamp ink
Felt
Hand-binding stapler
Sewing needles and pins

Punch or cut out a 3.5 x 2.5 inch (9 x 6.5 cm) rectangle out of the paper, fold it in half, and stamp something cute on the front. Punch or cut (using pinking shears) a 2 x 1.5 inch (5 x 3.5 cm) piece of felt. Affix the felt to the inside of the card using a staple. Insert the needles and pins into the felt. Done! The needle book can now go in the haberdashery bag.

CRAFT DATES—STYLING

One of the best things about organizing a Craft Date, if you ask me, besides thinking up a project and choosing the materials, is deciding on how to decorate and style everything for the day. Because there's nothing better than a nicely packaged project on a lovely table in an inspiring space.

You don't have to have a huge studio to organize a Craft Date. Just hosting one at home or in your backyard is totally fine. It is nice, though, to set up little styling areas with balls of wool, piles of fabric, beautiful books, and tools on display. Think, for example, of a large pot with knitting needles, a pair of scissors, and a ruler in it.

Hang up crochet garlands; place some crochet cushions and throws on a (garden) bench. Turn your home into a crafty space, being careful not to go overboard and fill the space up too much or make your décor too loud. It's a good idea to keep to a particular color palette. Limiting yourself to three or four colors will keep things stylish. Make sure things like napkins and tablecloths are in keeping with the color palette.

Having a tool station on the table is very handy, and you can customize the tool station and its contents for a particular Craft Date. Beautiful cards with inspiring texts or photos can be the perfect finishing touch for your table. Use a binder clip or a rustic bit of string to attach them to the project package or to a twig, branch, or stem on the table.

It is always nice to have a theme for a Craft Date. If you are planning to work with a sewing machine, using old patterns as packing material is a great option. Fill a glass pot with spools of sewing thread and place it on the table.

If you're planning a knitting or crochet project, consider placing baskets with small, self-wound balls of yarn on the table. If you have a wool winder, you can make yarn cakes very easily and arrange them on a strong skewer. This also allows you to personalize the colors of the yarn for each participant. It's that personal touch that really makes it fun.

Miriam

PETRA'S
CROCHET BASKET

DIAMETER 8.25 INCHES (21 CM), HEIGHT 4 INCHES (10 CM)

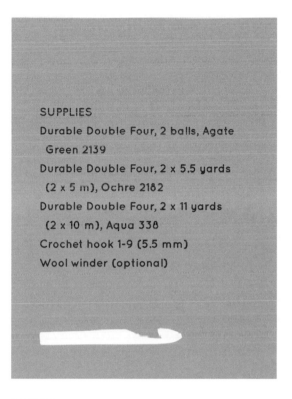

SUPPLIES
Durable Double Four, 2 balls, Agate
  Green 2139
Durable Double Four, 2 x 5.5 yards
  (2 x 5 m), Ochre 2182
Durable Double Four, 2 x 11 yards
  (2 x 10 m), Aqua 338
Crochet hook 1-9 (5.5 mm)
Wool winder (optional)

A strong, crochet basket like this is a handy and photogenic storage solution for balls of yarn, swaths of fabric, toiletries, or stationary.

INFO

This basket is crocheted using a double thread. You can do this by making two balls out of one ball using a wool winder. Alternatively, you can use two balls of Double Four. These are useful here because of the pull skein method used to wind the balls. This ensures that the yarn can easily be pulled from the middle.

METHOD

Row 1: Crochet using Agate Green and start with a magic ring, crochet 2 chains and 11 double crochets, and close the first row with a slip stitch in 2nd chain (12 double crochets in total).

Row 2: Crochet 2 chains, a double crochet in the same stitch, then 2 double crochets in every stitch (24 double crochets in total), and close the row with a slip stitch in the 2nd chain.

Row 3: Crochet 2 chains. *2 double crochets in the next stitch and 1 double crochet in the next stitch. *Repeat* * (36 double crochets in total). Close the row with a slip stitch in the 2nd chain.

Row 4: Crochet 2 chains, 1 double crochet in the next stitch. *2 double crochets in the next stitch and 1 double crochet in the next 2 stitches. *Repeat* * (48 double crochets in total). Close the row with a slip stitch in the 2nd chain.

Row 5: Crochet 2 chains, 1 double crochet in the next 2 stitches. * 2 double crochets in the next stitch, 1 double crochet in the next 3 stitches.

Repeat * (60 double crochets in total). Close the row with a slip stitch in the 2nd chain.

Row 6: Crochet 2 chains, 1 double crochet in the next 3 stitches. *2 double crochets in the next stitch, 1 double crochet in the next 4 stitches. *Repeat* * (72 double crochets in total). Close the row with a slip stitch in the 2nd chain.

Row 7: Crochet this row in the back loop of the previous row only, 1 chain, 1 single crochet in the next stitch; now, crochet 2 single crochets together by first taking a loop from the same stitch as the previous stitch and then pick the loop up in the next stitch. Repeat this until the end of the row. Do not close the row, keep crocheting round and round in a spiral.

Rows 8-11: From this row onward, crochet in both loops once again, repeat row 7, as the 1st stitch of row 8, and crochet the chain and the 1st single crochet of the previous row together. Keep crocheting in a spiral.

Rows 12 + 13: Repeat row 11 using Aqua.

Row 14: Repeat row 13 using Ochre.

Row 15: Repeat row 14 with Agate Green.

Row 16: Crochet slip stitches in the back loop only. Crochet very loosely; otherwise, the rim will be narrower than the basket. Close with a slip stitch in the 1st stitch and sew off all the threads.

You can easily make a smaller basket by crocheting one or two fewer rows for the bottom.

Lidy

Miriam

Bregje

HANDMADE
with love
by me

LIDY'S COAT RACK

FOR ALL OF YOUR HOMEMADE SCARVES

Scarves, you can never have enough of them! Most people who crochet like to crochet scarves, and seeing as you can't possibly wear them all at once, you'll also need a coat rack to hang them on. Make your own coat rack, for scarves or for so many other things.

SUPPLIES

Wooden plank

Sandpaper

Matte paint (Dekor Paint Soft from Pentart)

Masking tape

Hooks, screws, and a screwdriver

Hanging hooks for the back

Craft Dates stamps

METHOD

Sand the wooden plank, paying extra attention to smoothing the sawed-off edges.

Paint the plank. If you'd like to use different colors in different areas or add a pattern, you can do this by using masking tape to block off certain areas.

Screw in the hooks for the scarves into the plank. If you are doing this by hand, you can make a preliminary hole using a nail or the point of a screw. If you are using a power screwdriver, be careful to avoid splitting the wood.

Your coat rack is finished. Hang it on the wall with two screws or with hanging hooks affixed to the back of your coat rack.

Petra

Bregje

Miriam

PACKAGING INSPIRATION

Cover the table with a nice-looking vinyl table covering. Place the paint cans in a basket. Put out wooden planks for everyone, as well as a small glass jar for water with a paintbrush inside. Make a name label and lay it on the plank. Put all of the hooks together in a basket or container. This way, when everyone comes in, you can get straight to work.

MIRIAM'S PLACEMATS

Simple, colorful cotton placemats get a whole new look with these crochet details.

CUTLERY POCKET

Crochet 22 chains + 1 turning chain.

Row 1: Crochet 1 single crochet in each chain.

Row 2: Crochet 2 chains = 1st double crochet and then crochet 21 double crochets, 22 double crochets in total.

Repeat the second row 17 x, 18 rows of double crochets in total. Crochet 1 turning chain and crochet around it 1 single crochet in every double crochet. Using your 2nd color, crochet an edge consisting of single crochets at the top. Neatly, finish all of the loose threads.

NAPKIN HOLDER

Crochet 20 chains + 1 turning chain.

Row 1: Crochet 1 single crochet and 1 turning chain.

Row 2: Crochet 2 turning chains – 1st double crochet and then crochet 19 double crochets (20 double crochets in total).

Repeat row 2 twice.

Using your 2nd color, crochet an edge consisting of single crochets along the top. Neatly, finish all the loose threads.

Carefully pin the cutlery pocket in place on the placemat, 1.25 inches (3 cm) from the bottom edge and about 0.5 inch (1 cm) from the right-hand side. Stitch the sides and the bottom using a sewing machine or by hand. Pin the napkin holder on to the left side of the placemat at the same height as the cutlery pocket. Stitch the two sides to the placemat using a sewing machine or by hand.

RIBBON

Make a 0.5 inch (1 cm) fold on the short side of the ribbon and pin it on the right-hand side of your placemat about 0.5 to 0.75 inches (1 to 2 cm) above the bottom edge. Pin the ribbon a quarter of an inch (0.5 cm) over top of the bottom edge of the cutlery pocket. On the left-hand side, fold the end of the ribbon over the edge of the placemat.

Stitch the ribbon neatly on to the placemat. You can put a stamp on the ribbon if you'd like.

Pick out nice napkins and silverware and set your lovely table with your new placemats.

SUPPLIES

Cotton placemats (from IKEA, for example)

Durable Coral, 2 colors

Crochet hook, E-4 (3.5 mm)

Pins

Ribbon, 19.75 inches (50 cm)

Sewing machine (or needle and thread)

Darning needle

Craft Date stamps and stamp ink (optional)

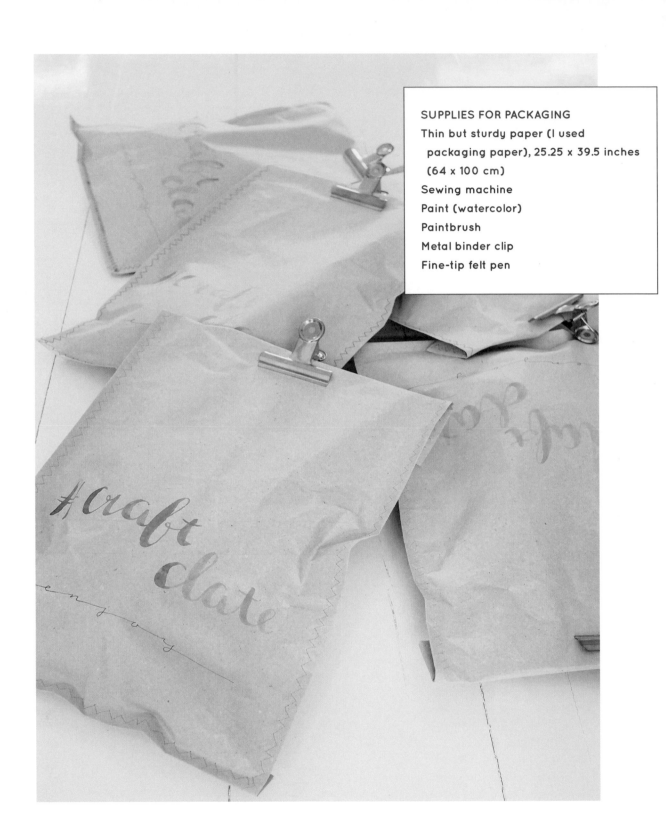

SUPPLIES FOR PACKAGING
Thin but sturdy paper (I used
 packaging paper), 25.25 x 39.5 inches
 (64 x 100 cm)
Sewing machine
Paint (watercolor)
Paintbrush
Metal binder clip
Fine-tip felt pen

PACKAGING INSPIRATION

To stylishly package up the materials, I made big "envelopes" out of thin, but sturdy (packaging) paper using the sewing machine.

Fold the paper in half, fold the bottom edge and the sides over about 0.75 inch (2 cm), and sew (using a sewing machine) these edges shut with a large, zig-zag stitch using black sewing machine thread.

Paint #CRAFTDATE on the envelope using watercolor paint and an interesting font. Underneath, write the word enjoy using a fine-tip marker.

Place the supplies for the project in the envelope and close it with a large, metal binder clip.

TIP
Buy a matching tea mug along with each color placemat and put it in the package. You could even add a nice set of wooden (disposable) cutlery and a fun, hip napkin.

Let's make stuff

MIRIAM'S QUICK SOUP

I thought up this soup myself one day. I'm no kitchen goddess, to be sure, but this soup is always a hit in our house. It's great for lunch or at the end of a fun Craft Date. The soup is easy to make and can be made in advance. Serve it in a nice bowl or even an empty jam jar. It's also a great addition to a buffet.

DIRECTIONS

Cut the chicken breast into small pieces.

Heat the olive oil in a soup pot and sauté the chicken in the oil.

Add the burrito seasoning mix and a bit of water, if the mixture is too dry.

Stir well and add the vegetable stock.

Bring to a simmer and then add the soup vegetables and chopped tomato.

Allow to simmer.

INGREDIENTS (serves about 6)
1 pound (approximately 500 g) chicken
   breast filet
Olive oil
1 packet (1.5 ounces, or 40 g) burrito
   seasoning mix
1 jar (4.2 ounces, or 120 g) of Maggi
   vegetable bouillon [Dutch brand]
1 large bag (28 ounces, or 795 g) of
   precut soup vegetables
3 tomatoes, chopped
3 to 4 cups (700 to 950 ml) water
1 package (26.5 ounces, or 750 g) of
   passata di pomodoro (strained tomato
   purée)
Salt and pepper
Fresh parsley

EQUIPTMENT:
Immersion blender
Clean tea towel

Remove the pot from the heat and purée using an immersion blender until smooth. To avoid splatters, drape a clean tea towel over the pot.

Return the pot to the stove and add more water (3 to 4 cups [700 to 950 ml]) so that you have a generous amount of soup.

Add the passata di pomodoro. Season to taste with salt and pepper.

Serve the soup in a bowl or jar and garnish with fresh parsley.

It's delicious with chunks of bread and breadsticks on the side.

Enjoy!

BREGJE'S XL INFINITY SCARF WITH A TWIST

CABLE KNITTING WITHOUT A CABLE NEEDLE—NICE AND FAST!

meet-share-create

The Durable Cosy XL or Durable Chunky yarn used in this variation on the infinity scarf gives it a lovely, robust texture.

You can make the scarf as long as you want. My example is 55 inches (140 cm) long and 11 inches (28 cm) wide. When sewn closed, I can wrap the scarf around my neck twice. It's perfect for a wintery walk in the forest or on the beach!

<table>
<tr><td>

SUPPLIES

Borgo de'Pazzi Emma 100% Wool, 3 balls

Knitting needles 15 to 17 (10 to 12 mm)

Embroidery needle

</td><td>

TIP

If you find that your woolen scarf is a bit on the itchy side, you can soak it in room-temperature water with a bit of hair conditioner (or mask) mixed in for 10 minutes. Rinse well and let it air dry on a towel.

</td></tr>
</table>

STITCH RATIO
12 stitches and 10 rows yield 4 x 4 inches (10 x 10 cm) knitted in the stitch pattern.

EDGE STITCH
On the right side: purl slip stitch with yarn back.
On the wrong side: purl slip stitch with yarn forward.

CABLE STITCH WITHOUT CABLE NEEDLE
Skip 1 stitch—do not slip, knit 2nd stitch—hold on the left needle, do not let it slip off. Knit 1st stitch, allow both stitches to slip off together.

Bregje's doubled up scarf

TIP
Miriam made her infinity scarf wider by casting on 40 stitches. She cast off when the height was 27.5 inches (70 cm). Sewn shut, she now wears it as a cozy extra large turtleneck.

A stamped label as accent.

Cast 34 stitches on (multiple of 3 plus 4 stitches).

Row 1 (wrong side)
1 edge stitch, * 2 purl, 1 knit, * repeat until the end of the needle. Note that the last stitch should be a purl instead of a knit.

Row 2 (right side)
1 edge stitch, * skip 1 stitch—do not slip—2nd stitch knit—hold on the left needle, knit the skipped stitch, allow both stitches to slip off together (= cable), 1 purl, repeat * * until there are 3 stitches on the left needle. Knit another cable; knit the last stitch instead of a purl.

Repeat rows 1 and 2 until your scarf is long enough. Sew the short ends together and your cozy infinity scarf is complete!

TIP
Wrap a bit of leftover yarn around the
original packaging of the wool you
used for your self-made treasures.
It's handy to keep washing
instructions and information on
the composition of the yarn.

SUPPLIES

Empty glass jars (with an opening of at least
  3.25 inches [8 cm] in diameter)
Plastic star stickers in various sizes
  (not paper!)
Matte paint
Paintbrush
Hair dryer (optional)
Tweezers or a pair of pincers
Wire, 25.5 inches (65 cm)
Combination pliers
Pencil
Remnants of leather, felt, paper,
  rope, buttons, etc.
Double-sided tape
Craft Date stamps and stamp ink
Embossing powder and heat tool
A handful of white sand (optional)
Tea lights

PETRA'S HURRICANE LIGHTS

MADE FROM JAM JARS

Stick the stars, divided evenly, on the jar, on the outside or the inside. (Sticking them on the outside is easier when it comes to removing the stickers after painting.)

Paint over the stickers and do not let the paint dry fully—use a hair dryer to speed things up if you'd like. Carefully remove the stickers using tweezers or a pair of pincers.

Take the piece of wire and wrap it around the pencil twice, making sure that you leave on one end a short side that is 6 inches (15 cm) long. Wind the two ends around the opening, pencil on the outside, and twist them closed. Trim the short end to about 0.75 inch (2 cm) and finish the end. Rotate the pencil once or twice more to ensure that the wire is tightly wrapped around the jar. Remove the pencil. Attach the long end to the "eye" that you made using the pencil. Twist the wire to finish it off.

You can leave the hurricane light as it is, or you can decorate it to your own taste with stamped twill tape, paper, ribbons, string, etc.

I made leather labels and used stamp ink and embossing powder to apply a raised stamp on them.

Fill the jar with a bit of white sand, if desired, and place a tea light inside.

PACKAGING INSPIRATION

Print your text using a printer on to paper sandwich bags and place the necessary materials in the bags. Take a piece of Kraft paper, 2.75 x 7 inches (7 x 18 cm), and fold it over the opening of the bag. Sew the piece of Kraft paper to attach it using a sewing machine.

SUPPLIES
Paper sandwich bags XL, 6.75 x 11.5 inches (17 x 29 cm)
Kraft paper
Extra thick thread (Gütermann ornamental stitch thread, for example)
Sewing machine

SUPPLIES

Book made of nice paper

(Double-sided) tape

Craft Date Stamps and
  stamp ink

Swatches of material

Cotter pins

Staples

Paper clips

Glue

Labels

Etc. Etc.

LIDY'S
CRAFT DATES INSPIRATION BOOK

LIDY'S CRAFT DATES INSPIRATION BOOK

If you do a lot of handiwork, are into creative things, and make a lot of projects, you'll probably take pictures of your work. We share lots of our successful projects on Instagram, Facebook, etc., which creates a sort of archive. But it's still nice to look back on the process as well. You can log all of this in this book: your inspiration, what you want to/are going to make, which materials you are going to use, which techniques. I personally enjoy the process of creating something—the journey to the finished product is so fun and interesting. I often can't recall exactly what I did to make something or how I came up with the idea in the first place.

You can record all of this in your book. Write down what you do, the sizes, technique, the tools you used, etc. I like to include samples of the materials I use, which can be done in so many different ways. Don't hold back and use materials and techniques that aren't standard. You can certainly just glue everything in, but you can also use staples, double-sided tape, paper clips, rivets, cotter pins, string, and threads to create a completely unique book that's filled with techniques. This is inspiring in and of itself!

This book gives you a good overview of everything you've made or of the plans you have. You can start a new book once every couple of years.

TIP
You can punch out the square holes seen here on the yarn cards using the Craft Dates die cutting template, see page 140.

SUPPLIES FOR THE CUSHIONS
Durable Cosy Fine, Mint (2137)
Knitting needles or (Tunisian) crochet hook
Waffle fabric in light green
Inner cushion
Darning needle

Cushions, from left to right: Bregje – Lidy – Miriam – Petra

GREEN YARN

KNIT AND CROCHET CUSHIONS, GARDEN GARLAND, AND RUG

During this particular Craft Date, the project wasn't the same for everyone, but the material was—light green yarn from Durable and matching waffle fabric.

The idea was for everyone to make a green cushion, but each in a different way. We ended up with a beautiful collection of cushions made with special crochet and knitting stitches.

Miriam crocheted the pattern for the round cushion using thick Hoooked Ribbon XL yarn, which led to a nice rug.

A lovely garden garland made of jute hung above the bench makes the image complete.

Miriam's round rug

Miriam's jute garland

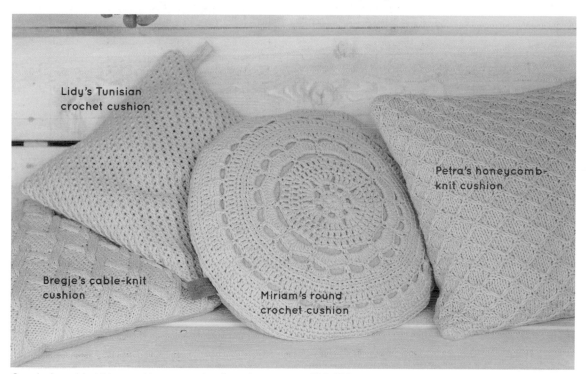

Lidy's Tunisian
crochet cushion

Petra's honeycomb-
knit cushion

Bregje's cable-knit
cushion

Miriam's round
crochet cushion

Crochet and knitting patterns can be found on pages 132–136.

Vary the length of the shoulder strap. Don't want a crossbody bag? Make the shoulder strap a bit shorter.

EAT
SLEEP
CRAFT
REPEAT

LIDY'S CROCHET BAG

See stitch diagram on page 76.

METHOD
Cast on: 38 chains.

Row 1:
Crochet your first double crochet in the
  5th chain.
Crochet a double crochet in every chain 33 x.
Crochet another 5 double crochets in the
  last chain.
Then, continue on the other side of the chains,
  crochet a double crochet in each chain, 33 x.
In the last chain, crochet 4 double crochets in
  your first 3 chains (76 double crochets
  in total).

Row 2:
Crochet 3 chains = 1st double crochet.
Crochet 1 double crochet on every double
  crochet, 33 x.
Crochet 2 double crochets on each of the next
  5 double crochets.
Crochet 1 double crochet on every double
  crochet, 33 x.
Crochet 2 double crochets on each of the next
  4 double crochets.
Crochet 1 double crochet in your first chains in
  the row and end the row with a slip
  stitch in the 3rd chain of the first chains
  (86 double crochets in total).

Row 3:
Crochet 3 chains = 1st double crochet.
Crochet 1 double crochet on every double
  crochet, 35 x.
Crochet 2 double crochets on each of the next
  6 double crochets.
Crochet 1 double crochet on every double
  crochet, 37 x.
Crochet 2 double crochets on each of the next
  6 double crochets.
Crochet 1 double crochet on the last double
  crochet and end the row with a slip stitch in the
  3rd chain of the first chains (98 double crochets
  in total).

SUPPLIES
DMC Natura Just Cotton, medium, 6 balls
Crochet hook G-6 (4 mm) or the size you
  need to achieve a tight crochet
Durable Coral in 6 colors for embroidery
Twill tape, 43.5 inches (110 cm), 0.75 to
  1.5 inches (2 to 3.5 cm) wide
Darning needle
Sewing machine (optional)
Pins
Embroidery stabilizer/backing, Vlieseline
  Stitch-n-Tear
Cotton for the lining, 19.75 inches (50 cm)
Vanishing fabric marker, pencil, or chalk
Iron

Lidy

Row 4:
Crochet 3 chains = 1st double crochet.
Crochet 1 double crochet on every double crochet, 36 x.
Crochet 2 double crochets on each of the next 3 double crochets.
Crochet 1 double crochet on the next 4 double crochets.
Crochet 2 double crochets on each of the next 3 double crochets.
Crochet 1 double crochet on every double crochet, 39 x.
Crochet 2 double crochets on each of the next 3 double crochets.
Crochet 1 double crochet on the next 4 double crochets.
Crochet 2 double crochets on each of the next 3 double crochets.
Crochet 1 double crochet on the next 2 double crochets and end the row with a slip stitch in the 3rd chain of the first chains (110 double crochets in total).

EMBROIDERED FLOWERS
Trace the pattern on to the Vlieseline Stitch-n-Tear using a vanishing fabric marker or a pencil. Pin the Stitch-n-Tear on to the bag. Now, embroider the flower on to the bag using Durable Coral. Use the satin stitch and chain stitch, as well as the Bullion knot. Carefully stretch and tear away the Stitch-n-Tear from the underside of your embroidery work.

Row 5:
Crochet 3 chains = 1st double crochet.
Crochet 1 double crochet on every double crochet, 38 x.
Crochet 2 double crochets on each of the next 3 double crochets.
Crochet 1 double crochet on the next 6 double crochets.
Crochet 2 double crochets on each of the next 3 double crochets.
Crochet 1 double crochet on every double crochet, 43 x.
Crochet 2 double crochets on each of the next 3 double crochets.
Crochet 1 double crochet on the next 6 double crochets.
Crochet 2 double crochets on each of the next 3 double crochets.
Crochet 1 double crochet on the last 4 double crochets and end the row with a slip stitch in the 3rd chain of the first chains (122 double crochets in total).

From Row 6 onward, crochet in a spiral until you achieve a height of about 13 inches (33 cm); lay your crochet work flat and measure from the midpoint of the bottom. Crochet the last 5 rows in single crochets to create a nice, tight edge.

SHOULDER STRAP
Crochet 9 chains.
Row 1: Start in the 5th chain from the hook and crochet a double crochet in each of the 5 chains. Turn your work.
Crochet 3 chains = 1st double crochet, crochet 5 double crochets, and repeat until the strap is long enough, about 43.5 inches (110 cm) long and 1.5 inches (4 cm) wide.
Stitch the twill tape on to the shoulder strap. Affix the tape by hand or using a sewing machine on the inside of the top edge 2 inches (5 cm) under the edge of the bag.

LINING

Fold the fabric in half. Lay the bag flat on top of the folded fabric. Trace the outline of the bag on to the fabric using chalk or a vanishing fabric marker. Cut along the lines on the fabric to make the lining. Stich together the sides and the bottom. Fold the uppermost edge 0.75 inch (2 cm) toward the "wrong" side of the fabric and iron it in place. Insert the lining into the bag, inside out, pin the lining in place just under the edge of the bag, and stitch it in place.

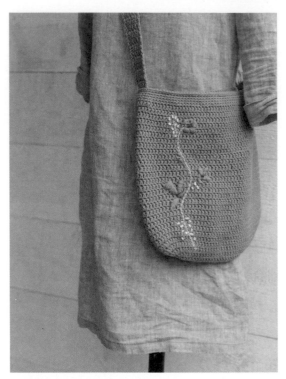

Bregje

Miriam

Petra

PACKAGING INSPIRATION

SUPPLIES
Paper gift bags
Cardstock label
Craft Dates stamps and stamp ink
Craft Dates patterned paper
String or ribbon

To neatly pack up the materials you'll need for the crochet bag, use ready-made, plain paper gift bags. Decorate one side of the gift bags using patterned paper and stamps. Gather the materials. Roll up the fabric for the lining and the twill tape. Place the balls of cotton and the other materials in the bag and add another piece of embroidery backing (Vlieseline Stitch-n-Tear). And don't forget the crochet pattern.

Pick out six colors of Durable Coral yarn per person for the embroidery work and wrap the strands around the cardstock labels. Hang the labels on the gift bags using string or ribbon.

Cast on 38 chains

Crochet pattern for the bottom of
Lidy's Crochet Bag

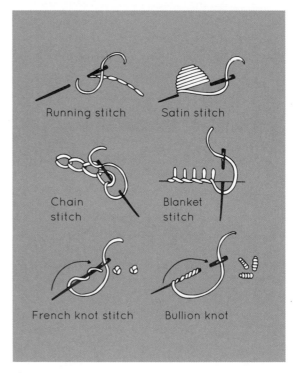

if i can't
take my
yarn
i'm not going

Imprint project bag, enlarge to 140%

Running stitch   Satin stitch

Chain
stitch   Blanket
                    stitch

French knot stitch   Bullion knot

Embroidery stitches

CRAFTINESS = HAPPINESS
HAPPINESS = HANDMADE

LIDY'S SLOW-STITCH WALL HANGER

Lidy

Embroidery is a voyage of discovery—just make a start and see where you end up. Don't make too many plans ahead of time. Add something and sometimes, take something away.

Slow stitch is an embroidery technique that arose from repair work. Using different bits of fabric and types of stitching, you repair holes in fabric and the extra stitching reinforces the fabric.

You stitch freehand; repetition is nice, but it doesn't all need to be so exact. Anything goes!

You can use this technique with clothing, but it's also nice to make a wall-hanging out of your work.

LIDY'S SLOW-STITCH WALL HANGER

You can lay out the bits of fabric for all your guests, or you can ask everyone to bring an assortment (of natural fabrics) to share with the group. You only need small pieces. Place them festively in a basket and let everyone cut off the pieces they need for his or her wall hanger. I always keep fabric remnants from projects in my "scrap fabric container" and they are perfect for this kind of project.

This was our fourth Craft Date project—a great way to spend the day. The slow stitch made us forget the time and, before we knew it, the day was already over.

TIP
Using fabrics with a gingham or plaid pattern and dots can help you embroider nice geometric figures and stitches, but working freehand is totally fine too! Stamp some images on the fabric. You can leave the images as is or accentuate them with stitching.

SUPPLIES
Embroidery hoop
DMC embroidery fabric
An assortment of bits of linen, cotton, and
  silk, plain or patterned (optional)
DMC embroidery thread, sewing thread
Embroidery needle with point
Craft Dates stamps and stamp ink
Pins
Sewing machine
Güttermann textile glue or double-sided
  tape (optional)

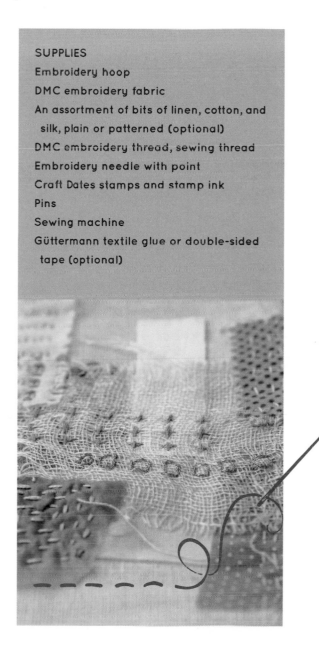

METHOD
Slow stitch—the name says it all—means stitching in a slow and relaxed way, by hand. Everything is allowed and anything goes! Don't hold back, let the process determine the final product.

Gather pieces of fabric and thread that appeal to you and look at them. Enjoy the colors and let yourself be inspired.

Secure your embroidery fabric in the embroidery hoop. Place the bits of fabric on the embroidery fabric so that they overlap. Make sure the pieces of fabric you use aren't too big. If you like what you see, pin the bits of fabric in place.

Take the embroidery fabric out of the hoop.

Now, you will begin sewing. Start with a running stitch, for example. It is nice if there is some repetition in the stitches, but this is by no means a hard and fast rule. Vary the stitch you use or the color thread.

Stitches used: see page 76.

Embroider with a hoop or without one; see what you prefer. Have a look at your work every so often, from a distance. If you're satisfied, it's time to finish it off.

Cut the embroidery fabric out so that it is 2 inches (5 cm) bigger in diameter than the embroidery hoop (you can use a plate or a lid to help you do this).

Stretch the fabric over the inner ring with the help of a needle and thread. Affix threads from one side to the other and stretch the fabric evenly around the ring. For the lining, cut out a circle that is 0.75 inch (2 cm) bigger in diameter than the ring.

Using a sewing machine, sew a large stitch 0.75 inch (2 cm) from the edge. Carefully pull the threads a bit to tighten them. The fabric will fold inward a little.

Fold the edge around the seam and pin the fabric on to the ring. Pin and correct for as long as it takes to get the lining to sit tightly against the fabric. Now, sew the lining, by hand, using small, invisible stitches. (Personally, this is something I enjoy doing, but if it doesn't seem achievable, just use Güttermann textile glue or double-sided tape to affix the lining to the fabric).

Attach the outside ring and hang your embroidery work on the wall.

Bregje

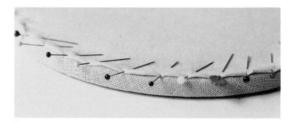

Miriam

Petra

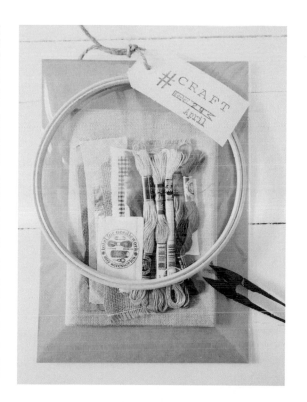

PACKAGING INSPIRATION

Make a nice composition with the materials; layer the bits of fabric on top of each other and place them on top of the embroidery fabric. Place the embroidery thread next to each other, on top of the fabric. Place the embroidery hoop on top and make a simple needle book (page 39) in a matching color. Place everything in a foil bag. Make a personal label and attach it to the bag with a piece of string.

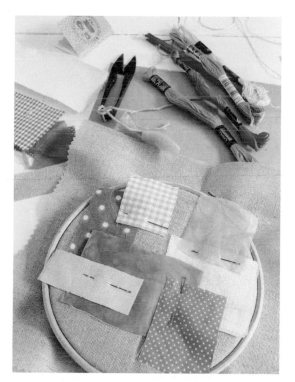

TOO MANY
IDEAS
NOT
ENOUGH
TIME

PETRA'S SALAD WITH CANDIED WALNUTS AND RASPBERRIES

This recipe was inspired by a recipe from Allerhande [Promotional material from a large Dutch supermarket chain]. I've since made my own version of this tasty salad, and it is always a hit with my family and friends. Everyone seems to find the candied walnuts particularly irresistible!

INGREDIENTS

½ cup (60 g) walnuts

1 heaping tablespoon (13 g) granulated sugar

1 tablespoon (15 ml) white wine vinegar

1 tablespoon (15 ml) sesame oil

2 tablespoons (28 ml) olive oil

Freshly ground black pepper

2 ripe avocados

1 bag (5 ounces, or 142 g) of mixed baby greens

1 small container (4.5 ounces, or 125 g) of raspberries

DIRECTIONS

Coarsely chop the walnuts. Heat a frying pan and add the walnuts and the sugar, stirring to combine. Melt the sugar on medium-high heat until it caramelizes, stirring occasionally to ensure that the walnuts are covered in a nice layer of sugar.

Allow the walnuts to cool on a plate.

(You can make the walnuts a day in advance if you'd like. But store them carefully because they are super tasty just on their own! You don't want casual snacking to leave you with less than you need when it comes time to make the recipe.)

Make a dressing from a tablespoon (15 ml) of white wine vinegar, a tablespoon (15 ml) of sesame oil, and two tablespoons (28 ml) of olive oil. Add a bit of freshly ground black pepper. You can also make this dressing ahead of time. Then, all you have to do during your Craft Date is cut up the avocado—super easy!

Spread out the greens on a nice plate, toss in the dressing, chop the avocados, and sprinkle them over the salad along with the raspberries. To finish, top with the candied walnuts.

PETRA'S
CHIC
SANDWICHES

Combining different flavors on slices of nice bread and adding a lettuce leaf is a quick way to make an ordinary sandwich chic. Here are two of my favorites that also happen to be ones that everyone asks for when I'm in charge of lunch.

ROAST BEEF WITH TUNA

INGREDIENTS
1 can (5 ounces, or 140 g) of tuna, packed in water
Mayonnaise
Freshly ground black pepper
5 pickles
Nice bread, light whole wheat
A few leaves of lettuce
Roast beef
Capers

DIRECTIONS
First, make the tuna salad: drain the tuna, remove the tuna from the can, and transfer it into a bowl using a fork. Combine with enough mayonnaise to make a creamy mixture. Season to taste with freshly ground black pepper. Finely chop the pickles and stir them into the tuna mixture.

Spread a bit of mayonnaise on the slices of bread and place a lettuce leaf and some roast beef on each one. Sprinkle with black pepper and top with a spoonful of tuna salad and a few capers. Close the sandwich with another slice of bread. Slice in half to serve.

AGED CHEESE AND FIG JAM

INGREDIENTS
Fig jam
Nice bread, dark whole wheat
Slices of aged cheese
A few leaves of lettuce

DIRECTIONS
Spread the fig jam on to the slices of bread, using two slices of bread per sandwich. On one half, place a lettuce leaf and two slices of aged cheese on top. Top with the other slice of bread and slice in half to serve.

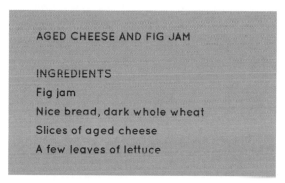

This is a very simple and
quick project that yields
great results, especially
when you add a few fresh
stems from the garden.

MIRIAM'S JUTE BOTTLE HANGER

SUPPLIES
Hoooked Natural Jute
Crochet hook, N/P-15 (10 mm)
Darning needle
3 empty (milk) bottles and flowers

We like Natural Jute from Hoooked because of the lovely colors on offer that match our color pallet perfectly. The jute is also 100% natural and fair trade.

Crochet 25 chains and 1 turning chain

Crochet 1 single crochet in every chain and at the end 4 chains, turn your work.

Crochet 1 double crochet in the 2nd single crochet in the back loop. Crochet 1 double crochet in the next single crochet in the front loop. Then, crochet alternating back and forth between 1 double crochet in the back loop, 1 double crochet in the front loop.

At the end of the row, crochet 4 chains and close with a slip stitch in the last single crochet.

You have now made two loops, one on either side, that can be used to hang up your work.

Cut 3 pieces of jute yarn, 15.75 inches (40 cm) long, and use them to tie the bottles to the bottle hanger. Tie the knots tightly. Hang up your creation, carefully fill the bottles with water, place a few fresh stems in the bottles, and enjoy your lovely, rustic flower hanger!

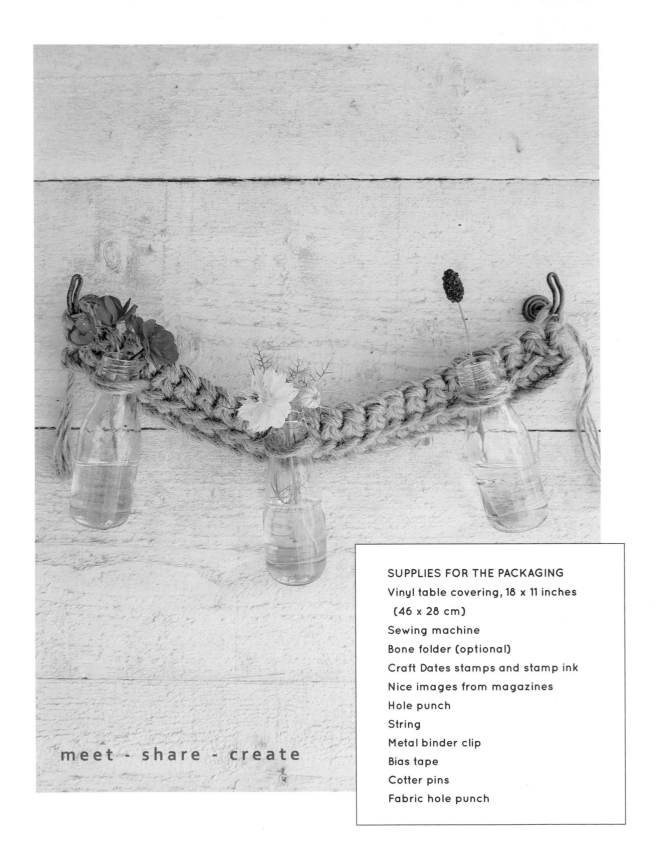

meet - share - create

SUPPLIES FOR THE PACKAGING
Vinyl table covering, 18 x 11 inches
 (46 x 28 cm)
Sewing machine
Bone folder (optional)
Craft Dates stamps and stamp ink
Nice images from magazines
Hole punch
String
Metal binder clip
Bias tape
Cotter pins
Fabric hole punch

PACKAGING INSPIRATION

To pack up the materials your guests will need to make their jute bottle hangers, I like to use pieces of vinyl table covering. The bag you make out of the vinyl can also be used to pack up a plant or to put a gift in.

METHOD

Fold the piece of table covering in half with the good sides facing each other. Stitch the side seam and the bottom closed using a sewing machine. Trim the corners and turn the bag right-side out. Press the corners out well—using a bone folder if you'd like (a super handy tool!).

Fold the top edge over about 1.5 inches (4 cm) and if you want, you can stamp a nice image on the edge to personalize your packaging. I always like to use beautiful images from magazines and folders—this time I've chosen matching garden images.

I've punched them out to make beautiful cards. Use a hole punch to make a hole in the cards, thread some string through the holes, and clip the string in place using the binder clips.

Place the bottles, the spools of jute from Hooooked, and the pattern in the bag. It's a great project for a summer Craft Date in the garden!

I bound the three empty bottles together using a length of bias tape. Measure off the length you'll need, make holes in the tape using a fabric hole punch, and attach the two ends of the tape (to make a loop) using the cotter pin.

Here's a handy apron that's easy to make. And it looks good too! The wrinkles that will appear from wearing it just make the linen prettier. Details like stitching and the placement of the pocket(s) and labels give your apron a unique look.

BREGJE'S APRON

MADE FROM BEAUTIFUL LINEN

SUPPLIES

A piece of linen or cotton, (49.25 inches)
125 cm for size S/M, 53.25 inches
(135 cm) for size L/XL
Matching sewing thread
Twill tape or decorative tape for label or
appliqué of choice
Pins

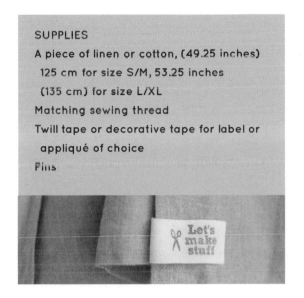

Cut the pieces in accordance with the sizes listed below. These include all the seams, hems, and appliqués.

A apron piece, 1 piece
S/M 35.5 inches (90 cm) long x 47.25 inches (120 cm) wide or
L/XL 39.5 inches (100 cm) long x 51.25 inches (130 cm) wide
B shoulder bands, 2 pieces 0.75 x 27.5 x 4.75 inches (2 x 70 x 12 cm)
C pocket, 1 piece 9.5 x 15 inches (24 x 38 cm)

Fold the shoulder bands in half, lengthwise, with the good side facing inward (= 27.5 x 2.5 inches [70 x 6 cm]). Stitch the long side closed with a 0.5 inch (1 cm) seam. Turn the band right-side out and iron it flat. Stich the sides of both straps, close to the edge.

Sew a double-fold hem, 0.75 x 0.5 inch (2 x 1 cm), on the sides of the apron piece. Fold the top edge 0.5 inch (1 cm) inward and then another 2.75 inches (7 cm). Baste this in place and then sew it in place.

Pin the shoulder bands where indicated (see pattern on page 93) behind the top edge. The bands cross over each other on the back. The right shoulder band should be sewn to the left corner. Make sure the band isn't twisted.

Make sure that the shoulder bands are the correct length for you. The average finished length of the bands is 23.75 inches (60 cm), but you might prefer them to be a bit longer or shorter. There is already 3.25 inches (8 cm) of extra fabric incorporated into the pattern for this purpose.

Finish the ends of the shoulder bands with a zig-zag stitch. Then, stitch the shoulder bands to attach them, making sure to reinforce the stitching for strength.

CRAFT
DATES

Sew nice!

Sew a double fold hem, 0.75 x 0.5 inch (2 x 1 cm), on the top edge of the pocket piece. Iron the side seams and the bottom of the pocket 0.5 inch (1 cm) inward.

If you'd like to add a label or something like that to the pocket, now is the time to stitch it in place. You can always iron something on later.

Pin and baste the pocket in place on the apron. Stitch on the pocket and stitch on a fun label sticking out of the side.

Sew a double-fold hem, 0.75 x 0.5 inch (2 x 1 cm), on the bottom edge of the apron.

You can personalize your apron even more by adding a fun label or a stamp, appliqué, and/ or decorative stitching. You could also consider attaching the pocket somewhere other than in the middle. It's up to you. We all did something a little bit different.

Have lots of sewing fun!

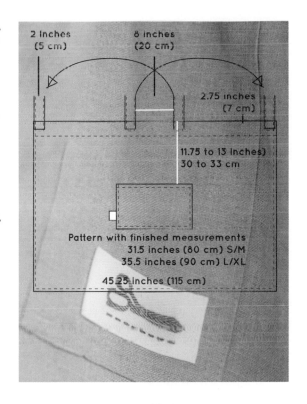

2 inches (5 cm)

8 inches (20 cm)

2.75 inches (7 cm)

11.75 to 13 inches) 30 to 33 cm

Pattern with finished measurements
31.5 inches (80 cm) S/M
35.5 inches (90 cm) L/XL
45.25 inches (115 cm)

Lidy

Petra

Miriam

PACKAGING INSPIRATION

SUPPLIES
Kraft paper envelope A4
White cardstock A5
Colored paper
Craft Dates die cutting templates
Craft Dates stamps and stamp ink
Old pattern paper or a photocopy
 of a pattern
Sewing thread
Paper tape
Metal binder clip
Vintage wooden clothespin
Felt pen or woodburning pen

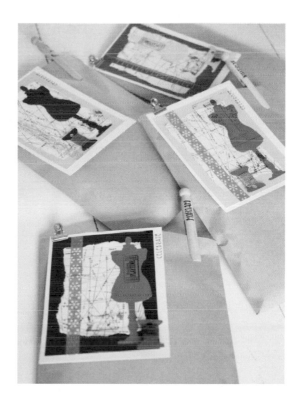

Stick a piece of colored paper on to the white card. Rip a piece of pattern paper in to an uneven square. Stamp or cut a mannequin or other figure out of colored paper, wrap a bit of thread around an embroidery card, and stick everything to the white card. Everything should match the color of the fabric for the apron, of course!

Place the fabric, thread, and the pattern in the large envelope. Put bits of twill tape for the labels and a neat button in a small bag.

You can attach the bag along with the card to the envelope using the metal binder clip. I used a woodburning pen to write the name of the recipient on the wooden clothespin, but you can also just use a felt pen. Clip the clothespin on to the envelope to finish it off.

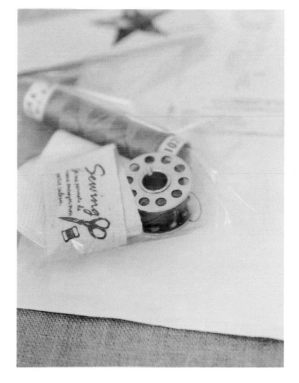

LIDY'S KNIT GARLAND

Just knit it!

A Craft Date is always a party if you ask us, and a party isn't complete without a garland. This garland isn't difficult to make and it's so nice to do—knitting and chatting go perfectly together. You can make one garland all together, or each of you can make your own in your favorite colors. Using the mini balls of yarn allow you to use lots of different colors, but you can also make smaller balls yourself. Pack the balls up for everyone individually or place all of the balls of yarn in a big basket on the table.

METHOD

You'll knit the flags with double yarn—one Durable Coral and one Durable Glam, together. Both yarns should be the same tint/color.

Stitches: Only knit.
Cast 20 stitches on to a size 10 (6 mm) knitting needle and knit 32 rows (= 16 garter stitches). Cast off and finish the yarns. Knit as many flags as you'd like.

Now, crochet (using a J-10 [6 mm] crochet hook), using the Durable Coral, a row of double crochets around three sides of each flag. Attach from the top side, crochet 3 chains and 1 double crochet in each garter stitch (16 x), on the corners, and crochet 4 double crochets. On the bottom edge, crochet 18 double crochets, 4 double crochets on the corner and 1 double crochet on every garter stitch (16 x), and then finish the yarns.

Once you've knit your flags and crocheted all of them on three sides, you will then crochet the flags to each other. Crochet 39.5 inches (100 cm) of chain stitches. Place your flags in the color order that you prefer; crochet them on with a single crochet in every chain on the flag. Crochet 15 chains and then attach the next flag. Keep going until you have attached all 7 flags. Now crochet 39.5 inches (100 cm) of chain stitches. Crochet a row of single crochets on to it using a 7 (4.5 mm) crochet hook. Finish the yarns.

Make tassels by wrapping one strand of Glam and one strand of Coral around a 4 inch (10 cm) wide piece of cardboard and cutting the strands loose on one side. Now, tie a two-strand tassel into every space in the crochet work on the underside of the flags. Fold the two strands in half, crochet the loop through the flag, and pull the ends through the loop.

Let the party start!

To make this multi-colored garland, I used 9 colors of Coral and Glam, but left-over bits of wool work just as well for this project!

Crochet
GOODNESS

A crochet scarf in your favorite color really is a must-have! This lovely version doesn't come to a point, but has a straight and a scalloped edge and can be worn a number of different ways!

MIRIAM'S CROCHET SCARF

INFO
This scarf is best when it feels nice and "chunky." See if your scarf turns out perfectly supple using a J-10 (6 mm) hook. If you want, you can use a larger hook or a smaller one if you tend to crochet quite loose.

SUPPLIES
Durable Cosy Fine, 6 balls, foundation color
Durable Cosy Fine or Durable Double Four, 1 ball in color of choice for the edging
Durable Glam or Durable Coral, 1 ball in 2nd color of choice for the edging
Crochet hook J-10 (6 mm)
Crochet hook H-8 (5 mm)
Optional: crochet hook 7 (4.5 mm) for the Durable Coral
Darning needle

Start with the foundation color and a J-10 (6 mm) crochet hook (if you tend to crochet tight, you may want to use a larger hook for the casting on row). Your casting on row should be about 15 inches (38 cm) wide.

Crochet 54 chain stitches.

Row 1: Crochet 1 double crochet in the 6th chain from the hook, skip one stitch, and crochet in the next stitch; 2 double crochets, 2 chains, 2 double crochets. * Skip 3 stitches and crochet in the next stitch; 2 double crochets, 2 chains, 2 double crochets, skip 3 stitches. * Repeat * * until you have 2 stitches left, skip 1 stitch, and crochet in the last chain 1 double crochet, 1 chain, 1 double crochet

Row 2: Crochet 6 chains (= 1 triple crochet + 2 chains). Crochet 2 double crochets, 2 chains, and 2 double crochets on the chains in the previous row. You will now crochet on to the chains from the previous row. Crochet 2 double crochets, 2 chains, 2 double crochets. * Repeat * *. In the last space, crochet 2 double crochets, 2 chains, 2 double crochets, 2 chains, 1 triple crochet.

Repeat the second row 25 x (26 rows in total).

Your scarf will now get wider on the sides. The scarf is now about 82.75 inches (210 cm) from end to end and about 15.75 inches (40 cm) wide in the middle.

Once you've crocheted all 26 rows (or have made the scarf as long and as wide as you want it to be), crochet a row of chains at the end. Then, crochet single crochets along the sides of your scarf (still in the foundation color Cosy Fine).

Crochet 4 single crochets on the triple crochets (see photo). And on the 2 chain spaces, crochet 3 single crochets. Close with a slip stitch in the 1st stitch of your edge.

On the wavy side of your scarf, stitch the Cosy Fine or Double Four on with a slip stitch (use crochet hook 5 now, if you'd like).

Now, crochet 2 single crochets on the chains. In the next 2 stitches, crochet 1 single crochet. Then, crochet 3 chains (above the 2 chain spaces) and in the next 2 stitches, 1 single crochet in each one. In the space between the double crochet groups, crochet 1 slip stitch. * In the next 2 stitches, crochet 1 single crochet, crochet 3 chains; in the next 2 stitches, crochet 1 single crochet; in the next space, crochet 1 slip stitch. * Repeat * * until the end of the wavy edge of your scarf. Crochet 1 single crochet in every single crochet on the straight edge of the scarf.

Stitch the Durable Glam or the Durable Coral on to the wavy edge (you may want to use an H-8 [4.5 mm] crochet hook here). In every stitch, crochet 1 single crochet; on the chain arc, crochet 3 single crochets. On the straight edge, crochet 1 single crochet in every stitch. Your scarf now has a straight edge and a wavy edge!

Finish all of the loose threads. Enjoy your scarf!

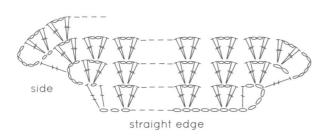

side

straight edge

PACKAGING INSPIRATION

SUPPLIES
Brown paper bags
Remnants Durable Cosy Fine
Crochet hook H-8 (5 mm)
Craft Dates stamps and stamp ink
Sewing machine
Hole punch

FLOWER
Crochet 7 chains and close with a slip stitch.

Row 1: Crochet 3 chains (= 1st double crochet), crochet 1 double crochet. * Crochet 6 chains, crochet 3 double crochets. * Repeat * * 4 x, crochet 1 double crochet, close with a slip stitch.

Row 2: Crochet 1 chain, crochet on the 6-chain arc. * Crochet 1 single crochet, 1 half double crochet, 6 double crochets, 1 half double crochet, 1 single crochet. Crochet 1 chain, 1 slip stitch on the 3 double crochets from the 1st row, 1 chain. * Repeat * * another 4 x.

Crochet 1 chain and close with a slip stitch.

Don't cut off your threads too short because you will use the ends to attach your crochet flower to the paper bag using paper tape or a clip.

You can also crochet a series of chain stitches upon which you can randomly make little bumps/details by attaching a few chain stitches together with a slip stitch. Hang this strand under your flower as a stem or vine.

PACKAGING
Crochet the flower and stem in your chosen color. Stamp the bag, place the balls of yarn in the bag along with the pattern, and sew the bag shut using the sewing machine. Fold the top neatly over.

Using the hole punch, make two holes, next to each other, in the bag. Tie the stem and the flower to the bag using the end threads.

TIP
It's a nice idea to use the same color yarn for the crochet flower and for the yarn you have put inside the bag for the project.

Lidy

Petra

BREGJE'S CRAFT CARDS

Cut and rip bits of paper, randomly, into different size pieces: long strips, small squares, wavy ripped lines.

Look for the nicest combinations of colors and textures. Watercolor paper, for example, has a lovely rough side and Vlieseline yields a nice fibrous edge if you rip it.

Position the pieces on top of each other or beside each other, overlapping slightly. Adjust things here and there until you achieve a nice-looking composition. You don't have to use everything, just using two of three pieces is enough to start. You'll see it when it's right for you.

When you're satisfied with how things look, stick the pieces to each other with a bit of glue to hold them in place. Sew the layers on top of each other using the sewing machine. You can sew along the edges, in a square, or zig-zag across the pieces. Try out sewing in a circle or even in a spiral.

Choose a piece of a map for someone who likes to travel or a line from an old, yellowed sheet of piano music. Combine that with a concrete print, in grey tints. Look for contrasts and subtle color combinations and you'll turn your cards into works of art.

Affix your sewn compositions to an appropriate-sized card. Finish it off with a nice stamp or a mother of pearl button or a bit of paper tape and pair it with a lovely envelope.

Bregje

There's no rules, no limitations! Let's get to work!

SUPPLIES
Packs of blank cards
Collection of nice paper, different types, textures, prints, and images, like Craft Dates design paper, watercolor paper, chalk paper, Vlieseline, old sheet music, an old atlas with country maps, magazines, etc.
Craft Dates stamps and stamp ink
Paper tape
Acid-free photo glue
Sewing thread in various colors
Sewing machine

Garland of leaves sewn together

Bregje

Miriam (leaf LR0478, punched from nice leather)

Lidy (a "real" thread through the stamped needle)

Bregje

This tart is deliciously fresh, so easy to make, and it doesn't even require an oven to make. You make it the night before— it needs a night to set. The tart is easy to take with you, and you can add the oh-so-essential finishing touch right before serving at your Craft Date!

BREGJE'S QUARK TART

DIRECTIONS

Line the bottom of a springform pan with parchment paper and clamp the ring around it.

Crumble the LU Bastogne cookies. Melt the butter in a saucepan. Stir the cookie crumbles into the melted butter.

Divide this mixture evenly across the bottom of the springform pan to make the crust. Press it down firmly using the back of a spoon. Place the pan in the fridge.

Soak the gelatin sheets in water for about 5 minutes.

Drain the mandarin segments and keep a half a cup (120 ml) of the juices. Heat the juice in a saucepan. Dissolve the gelatin sheets in the juice and allow the mixture to cool (consult the package instructions, as well).

Beat the whipping cream with the sugar and vanilla until it forms peaks. Stir in the dissolved gelatin mixture, the quark, and the lemon juice. Add the mandarin segments last, stirring gently to combine.

Pour the quark filling on to the well-cooled crust. Shake the pan gently to ensure that the filling is evenly distributed. Place the tart in the fridge overnight to set. (I like to cover the pan with plastic wrap and then put a pot lid on top to protect it.)

Right before serving, sprinkle the top of the cake with red fruits—thawed on time—nice and messy on top of the white tart.

Done and enjoy!

INGREDIENTS (serves about 12)

For the crust:
7 ounces (200 g) LU Bastogne cookies
5½ tablespoons (75 g) butter or margarine

For the filling:
4 sheets of white gelatin
1 can (11 ounces, or 312 g) of mandarin segments
9 ounces (250 ml) whipping cream
⅔ cup (125 g) white cane sugar
1 teaspoon vanilla
17.5 ounces (500 g) low-fat quark or Greek yogurt
Juice of 1 lemon
1 package (5 ounces, or 142 g) of frozen mixed berries, thawed to serve

EQUIPMENT
Round springform pan with a 9.5 inch (24 cm) diameter
Parchment paper

Petra

PETRA'S OILSKIN PROJECT BAG

SUPPLIES

Piece of oilskin, 19.75 x 55 inches (50 x 140 cm) (available for purchase at Stik 'n Stof)

Cotton, canvas, or sturdy linen for the lining, at least 19.75 x 43.25 inches (50 x 110 cm)

Sewing machine

90/14 denim sewing machine needle

Clover Wonder Clips (3155)

Prym magnetic snap in antique brass

Prym bronze-colored studs, 3 pieces

Cotton twill tape, for bag handles, 32.25 x 1 to
 1.25 inch (82 x 2.5 to 3 cm)

I think oilskin is a beautiful material. It is oiled cotton with a rugged appearance and whenever you make something out of it, it always looks super professional. It is greasy, impregnated with oil to make it water resistant, which means that the oil from the fabric can transfer a bit in the beginning, but this goes away with time and use.

Oilskin cannot be ironed, but it folds very well. When you use the bag, you'll see the folds and creases, but this is precisely what I love about the material!

Lidy folded the hem of the external pockets outward instead of inward.

CUTTING

Cut the following pieces to size; the following includes a 0.5 inch (1 cm) seam.

From the oilskin (outer fabric):
Two x 10.75 x 14.5 inches (27 x 37 cm) (A)
One x 7 x 14.5 inches (18 x 37 cm) (B)
Two x 2.75 x 14.5 inches (7 x 37 cm) (C)
One x 6.75 x 34.25 inches (17 x 87) (D)
Two x 2.75 x 6.75 inches (7 x 17) (E)

From the lining fabric:
Two x 8.75 x 14.5 inches (22 x 37 cm)
One x 6.75 x 30.25 inches (17 x 77 cm)

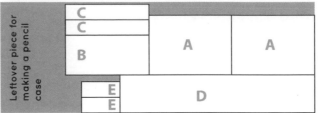

Cutting pattern outer fabric

19.75 inches (50 cm)

55 inches (140 cm)

2 x A = 14.5 x 10.75 inches (37 x 27 cm)
B = 14.5 x 7 inches (37 x 18 cm)
2 x C = 14.4 x 2.75 inches (37 x 7 cm)
D = 34.25 x 6.75 inches (87 x 17 cm)
2 x E = 2.75 x 6.75 inches (7 x 17 cm)

For the handles, cut two 16.25 inch (41 cm) lengths of twill tape.

SEWING

Set up your sewing machine with a denim needle 90/14 before you start sewing the bag.
Use stitch length 3.

With oilskin, using pins is not a good option, as the holes they make will remain visible in the fabric. This is why I suggest using Wonder Clips from Clover. They are little clamps (a sort of clothes peg) that allow you to affix layers of fabric to each other. They are also handy if you are working with a vinyl table covering.

Miriam sewed an extra pocket on the outside and also added a robust twill tape loop.

Take the 7 x 14.5 inch (18 x 37 cm) piece of outer fabric, fold the uppermost edge 0.75 x 0.5 inch (2 x 1 cm) toward the inside (toward the reverse side of the fabric) and stitch it in place along the edge.

Sew this piece, with a narrow seam on the sides, to the good side of the front piece of the outside of the bag (one of the 10.75 x 14.5 inch [27 x 37 cm] pieces). Now, sew this piece through the middle to attach it—this will form two pockets. Reinforce the seam by sewing back and forth a couple of times at either end.

Attach this front of the bag in the middle of the long piece (6.75 x 34.25 inches [17 x 87 cm]) with a 0.5 inch (1 cm) seam, with the good sides facing each other. Start and finish the stitching 0.5 inch (1 cm) from the side. Now, attach the back of the bag in the same way on the other side of the long piece.

Clip the side seam on one side in place with the Wonder Clips. Make a small cut here in the long piece where the bottom corner is formed, diagonal to where you started the seam for the underside. Repeat this on the other side.

Stitch the side seams with a 0.5 inch (1 cm) seam and sew back and forth twice over the area that you trimmed off. Repeat this on the other side. Reinforce the corners on the front of the bag with studs, one on each side and one above the middle seam. The outside of the bag is now finished.

Now, put the lining of the bag together. First, sew the narrow edges of the oilskin on to the top edge of the lining fabric—on both ends of the narrow strip and on the top edges of the front and back of the bag.

Continue sewing the lining in the same way that you sewed the bag, but leave 4 inches (10 cm) open on one side of the seam on the bottom. You will use this opening to turn the bag right-side out.

Bregje made several storage pockets in her lining.

Sew in place the magnetic snap in the middle of the top of the inside lining. Use a double layer of fabric to reinforce the closure on the back.

The bottom of the closure is 0.75 inch (1.7 cm) from the bottom edge where the lining fabric meets and is attached to the outer fabric.

Place the handles in the middle of the good sides of the outer fabric and keep them in place using the Wonder Clips. The handles should point downward. The space between both sides is 4.75 inches (12 cm).

Turn the lining bag so that the good sides face inward; place the outer fabric bag in the lining bag with the good sides facing each other. Stitch all the way around and stitch back and forth 3 x over the handles. Turn the bag right-side out using the opening in the bottom of the lining bag. Sew the opening in the lining closed. Fold the top edge and stitch closely along the edge.

PACKAGING INSPIRATION

SUPPLIES
Brown cardboard mailing box
Red and white ribbon
Small hanging labels
Black cardstock
Craft Dates die cutting template,
 scissors (COL1445)
Letter stamps

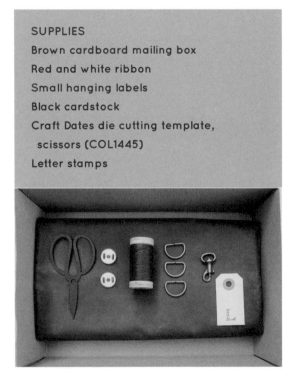

Place all of the materials in the box. Stamp the initial of the recipient on to the small label. Punch a pair of scissors out of black cardstock. Tie the ribbon around the box and attach the label and the scissors by the knot. Cut the ends of the ribbon diagonally so that they are about 2 inches (5 cm) long.

PETRA'S PROJECT BAG

PETRA'S PROJECT BAG WITH IMPRINT

METHOD

To make the bags, cut out 13.75 x 29.5 inch (35 x 75 cm) pieces of unbleached cotton. Finish the long sides with a zig-zag stitch. Fold the piece of fabric in half, lengthwise.

Sew one side closed to 2.5 inches (6 cm) from the top and the other side completely closed. Sew the seam allowance to the top of the open top side. Fold this top side 0.5 inch (1 cm) inward and then 0.75 inch (2 cm) inward. Sew along this edge and then again 0.5 inch (1 cm) from the top edge. Thread the twill tape through the tunnel.

Cut the self-adhesive template using a cutting plotter or transfer the mirror image of your text to the back side of the template using a sharp hobby knife.

Use the transfer tape or masking tape to affix loose pieces in the letters (if necessary) so that they can also be transferred to the fabric.

SUPPLIES

Unbleached cotton (13.75 x 29.5 inches [35 x 75 cm] for 1 bag), or ready-made canvas bags

Sewing machine (only when making your own bags)

Twill tape (only when making your own bags)

Vinyl foil or adhesive backed stencil sheets

Cutting plotter (like Silhouette Cameo) or a sharp hobby knife

Transfer tape or masking tape

Plastic (bank) card or squeegee

Paint samples with roller (or leftover paint and a foam brush)

Printer paper or cardstock (to prevent the paint from bleeding through)

Tweezers or small hook

Parchment paper (optional)

Iron (optional)

Place the printer paper or the cardstock in the bag. Stick the stencil to the fabric; use a plastic card or a squeegee to get the loose pieces in the letters printed on the fabric.

Carefully remove the transfer or masking tape from the stencil and use the paint roller (or foam brush) to color in the open areas of the stencil, thereby printing the text on to the fabric. Use the tweezers or a small hook to remove the loose pieces from the letters.

Allow to dry and set the imprint, if you wish, by laying parchment paper over the imprint and going over it with a warm iron.

PACKAGING INSPIRATION

SUPPLIES
Large Kraft envelopes
Leftover bits of design paper
Paper doily
Paper hanging label
Colored index cards (stationary store)
Piece of lace or ribbon, 11.75 inches
  (30 cm)
Piece of string
Craft Dates stamps and stamp ink
Stapler

Stamp or write the name of the recipient on to the labels (I used my cutting plotter to punch the names on the labels), tie the string around the label, and stamp an image on the index card. Place all the materials for the project in the envelope.

Rip off a strip of design paper and fold it over the top edge of the envelope, together with the paper doily. Take the label, the index card, and the piece of lace, put them together, and staple them to the top of the envelope.

SUPPLIES

3.5 ounces (100 g) white
  wool, for example Regia
  Superwash sock wool
Plastic gloves
Plastic sheeting
Roll of plastic cling wrap
Glass jars
Distilled white vinegar (not
  cleaning vinegar)
Food coloring in a variety
  of colors (for example,
  Wilton)
Spoons
Paper towels
Plastic microwave-safe
  container
Two cloth towels
Household sponges or
  hobby sponges on a stick

TIP
If you wind two yarns together in
one skein, you will end up with two
identical balls of wool. This is helpful
if you want to knit two of the same
socks, mittens, or muffs.

DYING YARN

With a while ball of wool and a little food coloring, you can very easily create wool in your favorite colors. It's simple to do in your own kitchen, using the microwave!

Choose yarn made of wool or a wool-polyester mix, like sock wool (70% wool/30% polyester). Superwash yarns are even machine washable. The dye we use is food coloring. It's readily available online, in baking stores, or at Xenos [a Dutch chain of stores]. It is available in paste and liquid forms. The latter is easiest to dissolve in water. It is available in a wide variety of colors, and the best part is that it is nontoxic.

This dye won't work on cotton or other natural fibers, but it works for wool; it is colorfast and washable—not too hot, of course! It's still wool!

We used different yarns and used a wool winder to make a skein. You can also do this using the backs of two chairs or around two table clamps. Make sure the skein is at least 3 feet 3.25 inches (1 m) long and 6 feet 6.75 inches (2 m) in circumference.
Tie the skein off at 4 points with a piece of cotton yarn to prevent it from getting tangled.

Mix 1 quart (1 L) of lukewarm water with 3.5 ounces (100 ml) of vinegar and soak the skein of wool in this mixture for at least a half an hour. Meanwhile, you can set up your jars of dye.

TIP
If you are dying yarn for the
first time, you should start with
Superwash sock wool. It yields
the best result.

First, put on your plastic gloves. Protect your table with plastic sheeting. Place a piece of plastic wrap on the table that is a bit longer than your skein.

Fill the glass jar half full with water/vinegar solution (3.5 ounces [100 ml] vinegar to 1 gallon [1 L] warm water). Spoon a pea-sized amount of food coloring out of the jar. If you are using liquid food coloring, start with about 10 drops. Dissolve the food coloring in the jar with the water/vinegar solution. Stir well to ensure that the food coloring has dissolved. Stick a bit of paper towel in the solution to see if you are happy with the intensity of the color. Add a bit more food coloring for a deeper color or more water for a more pastel tint. Keep in mind that excess dye won't be absorbed by the wool. The colors will then run into each other in the microwave.

Use this method to mix all of the colors you want to use.

Remove your soaked wool and squeeze the liquid out. You can give it a spin in your salad spinner to dry it further if you'd like, we are in the kitchen after all! Wrap the wool in a towel and squeeze out any remaining water.

Lay the skein of wool on the plastic wrap on the table, in an oval. Make sure that the edges of the plastic exceed the length of the wool enough so that you can wrap the wool in the plastic later on.

Place the jars of dye on the table with a sponge for each color.

Dip the sponge in the dye solution and carefully dab the wool. The dye should not be allowed to run to the underside of the wool. Everything you dab on should be absorbed by the wool. Make sure you color the underside and inside of the wool as well.

Only add the next color when you have done this. If you don't want the colors to run into each other, keep about 0.75 inch (2 cm) of white wool between the colors.

Use this method to apply all of the colors. Make stripes or color half in one color and half in another, make big (or small) spatters with the help of skewers, or let the colors run from dark to light!

When you are done and satisfied, wipe away as much water from the plastic as you can, using paper towels. It should only be water as the wool will have absorbed the dye. If there is still a fair amount of color in the water under your skein, you probably used too much dye in your solution. In this case, try to wipe away as much of the dye as possible or massage it into the wool.

Fold the plastic wrap closed around the skein lengthwise. Fold the ends in to close them as well. Now, you can carefully roll up your skein. Place the skein in a microwave-safe container.

Place the container in the microwave (800 watts) for 3 minutes.

The water that runs out of the skein should be clear. Heat it a minute longer, if necessary. Allow the skein to cool fully before removing it from the plastic wrap. Watch out! The steam that comes out is very hot!

Rinse the cooled skein well in lukewarm water, with a drop of dish soap, if you wish. The water should be completely clear of dye.

Squeeze the water out of the skein—don't wring it! Roll up the wool in a dry towel and press out any remaining water. Hang the skein up to dry fully.

Good luck!

Wraps and labels made with Craft Dates stamps and die cutting templates.

PACKAGING INSPIRATION

SUPPLIES

**Square or rectangular cookie tins
(thrift store)**

Spray paint in a variety of colors

Craft Dates stamps and stamp ink

**Remnants of wallpaper or wrapping
paper**

Paper label

Self-drying clay

Cookie cutter

Metal binder clip

Embroidery piercing tool

Stapler

Clean and degrease the cookie tins. Spray paint the lids and bottoms in different colors. Allow to dry fully.

Stamp a couple of motifs on to the lids. Place the materials for your project into the tins—wool, dye, plastic gloves, etc. Write the name of each recipient on the labels.

Use a large piece of wallpaper to make a bag—the tin should fit into the bag. Place the tin in the paper bag. Staple the bag closed and attach the name label to the bag.

Attach a paper label together with a nice, clay label to the bag. The clay label can be made by rolling out the clay and using a cookie cutter to make a shape. Stamp an image on to the still-wet clay (without ink), make a hole in the top, and let the clay dry.

The paper label is made by punching holes in the paper with an embroidery piercing tool and adding crochet around the edges.

LIDY'S
PENCIL CASE

While the cases may be all the
same form, they are all made from
different materials, creating handy
pencil cases for your telephone,
glasses, pens, or crochet hooks.

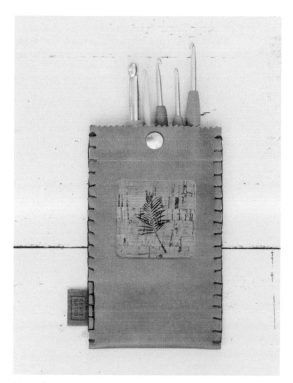

Lidy: leather

Petra: felt

Bregje: cork

Miriam: canvas

LIDY'S LEATHER PENCIL CASE

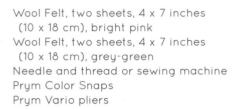

SUPPLIES
Flannel
Vliesofix Bondaweb fusible
 web paper
Iron
A piece of leather, 4.25 x 14.5 inches (11 x 37 cm)
Rotary cutter Textile glue (such as Güttermann)
Fabric hole punch
Ruler
Durable thin crochet/embroidery cotton
Piece of ribbon
Craft Dates stamp and stamp ink
Pinking shears
Snap closure
Prym Vario pliers

METHOD
Cut a 4.25 x 14.5 inch (11 x 37 cm) piece of leather.
Cut a 4.25 x 14.25 inch (11 x 36 cm) strip of flannel.
Cut a 4.25 x 14.25 inch (11 x 36 cm) strip of Bondaweb.

Iron the flannel on to the Bondaweb. Trim the flannel down to 4 x 13.75 inch (10 x 35 cm). Use a damp
 cloth when ironing the Bondaweb. Cut or punch out
 a square in the middle of the leather, 2 inches (5 cm)
 from the top edge.
Stamp a piece of cork that is a bit bigger than the
 square hole you just cut. Use double-sided tape to
 affix the cork to the inside of the window. Iron the
 flannel to the back of the leather and over the piece
 of cork, making sure that you leave 0.5 inch (1 cm)
 free on both of the long sides.
Fold the leather in half and affix the sides to each
 other with a little bit of glue.
Using the fabric hole punch, make holes in the leather that are of equal distance apart, such as 0.5 inch
 (1 cm); use a ruler to plot where the holes should
 be. Using a festoon stitch, close the sides using a
 double thread. Stitch the threads inward and glue
 them down with a bit of glue.
Make a label from a bit of ribbon and a stamp, fold
 this in half, and cut the sides evenly with pinking
 shears. Place the label on the side, under your pencil
 case, and stitch it in place. Now, attach the snap at
 the top in the middle, about 0.5 inch (1 cm) from
 the edge.

PETRA'S FELT PENCIL CASE

SUPPLIES
Small piece of Vliesofix Bondaweb fusible web paper
Iron

Wool Felt, two sheets, 4 x 7 inches
 (10 x 18 cm), bright pink
Wool Felt, two sheets, 4 x 7 inches
 (10 x 18 cm), grey-green
Needle and thread or sewing machine
Prym Color Snaps
Prym Vario pliers

METHOD
Trace a flower on the piece of Bondaweb . Iron it to
 one of the pieces of grey-green felt, according to
 the instructions, so that the flower is just under the
 middle.
Cut out the flower. Remove the paper from the
 Bondaweb and iron the green felt on to one of the
 pieces of pink felt. Use a festoon stitch to finish the
 top edge.
Lay the other two pieces of felt on top of each other
 and stitch, using a festoon stitch once again (I used
 the sewing machine, but you can also do this by
 hand), the short, top edge together.
Lay the pieces with the pink sides on top of each
 other and sew the sides and bottom closed with a
 festoon stitch.
Finish with a Color Snap as closure on the top.

BREGJE'S CORK PENCIL CASE

SUPPLIES
Cork leather (cork fabric), 15.75
 (40 cm) long x 3.5 inches (9 cm) wide
Leather remnant
Vliesofix Bondaweb fusible web paper
Piece of flannel, 14.5 x 3.5 inches
 (37 x 9 cm) for the lining
Iron
Textile glue (such as Güttermann)
Sewing machine or needle and thread
Twill tape or ribbon
Craft Dates stamps and stamp ink
Clover Wonder Clips
Prym Color Snaps
Prym Vario pliers

METHOD
Punch or cut out a star shape in the cork, about 4.75
 inches (12 cm) from the top (the narrow side). Stick
 a piece of leather or fabric behind the cut-out star
 that is just a bit bigger than the star. Stitch this in
 place, neatly around the edges.
Iron the Bondaweb on the reverse side of the flannel, in accordance with the package instructions.
 The flannel is 0.5 inch (1.5 cm) shorter on both short
 sides than the cork. Fold the short ends of the cork

inward and affix with a bit of glue on the flannel. Sew a decorative trim out of twill tape or ribbon along the top edge. Before you sew it on, stamp something nice on to the tape.

Fold the case in half, lengthwise, with the good side facing outward. Hold it in place using a couple of Wonder Clips. These will keep the layers of fabric in place without pricking holes in the cork. While you're sewing, remove the clips, one by one.

To make a label, cut a small, 0.75 x 0.75 inch (2 x 2 cm) square out of leather. Fold it in half with the good side facing outward. Stamp a small image on to it. Insert it 0.5 inch (1 cm) into your side seam, where you want to place it. Affix it with a bit of glue before you sew, so it doesn't slide around. Sew the sides closed, as close to the edge as possible. Stitch the label in place.

Attach the Color Snap closure, centered in the middle of the top edge.

Slide in your sunglasses and you're done!

MIRIAM'S CANVAS PENCIL CASE

SUPPLIES
Piece of oilskin, 3.5 x 10.25 inches
 (9 x 26 cm)
Piece of canvas, 6.75 x 10.25 inches
 (17 x 26 cm)
Sewing machine and thread
Vliesofix Bondaweb fusible
 web paper
Piece of flannel, 5.25 x 15.75 inches
 (13 x 40 cm)
Iron
Pins
Twill tape, 1.25 x 15.75 cm (3 x 40 cm)
Bone folder (optional)
Fabric hole punch
Prym Color Snap
Prym Vario pliers
Craft Dates stamp and stamp ink (optional)

METHOD
Sew everything with a 0.5 inch (1 cm) seam.

Lay the oilskin on the canvas with the good sides facing inward (toward each other). Sew the oilskin to the canvas on the short sides, iron the seams open, and stitch them neatly on the good side. You should now have a piece of fabric that is 15.75 inches (40 cm) long and 5.25 inches (13 cm) wide.

Iron the Bondaweb on to the piece of flannel. Remove the paper from the Bondaweb and lay it with the sticky-side down on the reverse side of the piece of canvas/oilskin. Iron carefully to affix the fabric and let the pieces rest for a minute.

Pin the twill tape to the canvas, 1.5 inches (4 cm) above the oilskin, and stitch it neatly in place. Pin the tape along the top edge of the good side, 0.5 inch (1 cm) from the edge and fold it over the top edge toward the inside. Stitch it in place all at once. Lay the case with the good sides on top of each other and sew the sides closed. Iron the seams open and turn your case right-side out. Carefully fold out the corners, using a bone folder if necessary.

Use a fabric hole punch to make holes in both top sides (0.5 inch [1 cm] below the top edge) and affix a Color Snap closure. If you'd like, you can place a stamp on the twill tape and of the reverse side.

It's a great case for my cell phone—the soft flannel ensures that my phone stays scratch-free!

PACKAGING INSPIRATION

SUPPLIES
Tin cans
Paper bags

Roll the materials (fabric, cork, felt, leather, tape) and place them in the can in a decorative way. Stamp the bag and place the smaller accessories (like the Color Snap closures) in the bag. Hang a nice, cork label on the can using string or ribbon.

THIS IS HOW WE CROCHET A BLANKET

The blanket is made up of a total of 64 granny squares—16 of each design and if you're making them with a group of four people, that makes 16 per person.

To achieve a nice distribution of design and color in the blanket, each person should crochet the following:
- 4 one-color granny squares
- 4 two-color granny squares, change color after row 1
- 4 three-color granny squares, change color after row 1 and row 2
- 4 four-color granny squares, change color after rows 1, 2, and 3

PETRA'S LACE GRANNY SQUARE

Row 1: Start with a magic ring, crochet 8 single crochets, and end with a slip stitch in the first single crochet.

Row 2: 2 chains, 1 double crochet. * 4 chains, cluster of 2 double crochets, 2 chains, cluster of 2 double crochets. * Repeat * * 2 x. Crochet 4 chains, cluster of 2 double crochets, 2 chains, a slip stitch in the second beginning chain.

Row 3: 2 chains, this is the first double crochet in a cluster of 4 double crochets. * 4 chains, cluster of 4 double crochets, 3 chains, cluster of 4 double crochets. * Repeat * * 3 x. Finish with a slip stitch in the top of the first cluster of 4 double crochets.

Row 4: In the space of 4 chains in the previous row, crochet: 1 slip stitch, 4 chains * (this is 1 double crochet and 2 chains), 1 double crochet, 3 chains, 1 double crochet, 2 chains, 1 double crochet. 4 chains, 1 single crochet in the space of 3 chains in the previous row, 5 chains, 1 single crochet in the space of 3 chains in the previous row, 4 chains. * Repeat * * 3 x. Finish with a slip stitch in the 2nd chain of the 4 beginning chains.

Row 5: In the corners, crochet 3 double crochets, 2 chains, 3 double crochets, in the leftover space, keep crocheting 1 double crochet with a chain in between. Start with a slip stitch and 3 chains and end with a slip stitch in the 2nd of the beginning chains.

Row 6: Crochet a double crochet in every double crochet and chain space in the previous row. In the corners, crochet: 2 double crochets, 2 chains, 2 double crochets. Start with 2 chains and end with a slip stitch in the 2nd of the beginning chains.

Row 7: Using your joining color, crochet a double crochet in every double crochet in the previous row, in the corners 2 double crochets, 2 chains, 2 double crochets. Start with 2 chains and end with a slip stitch in the 2nd of the beginning chains.

MIRIAM'S TRADITIONAL GRANNY SQUARE

This is the basic pattern for a granny square and it just happens to be my favorite! If you can crochet this, the possibilities are endless in terms of color and execution! Cushions, blankets, scarves . . . with fine or thick yarn. That's why this classic is my contribution to the blanket. This pattern is written out in full, which makes it well-suited to beginners.

Crochet 4 chains and close with a slip stitch. Crochet your beginning yarn into your first row; this will allow you to pull it nice and tight later on. With this granny square, you will need to turn your work after every row!

Row 1: Crochet 3 chains (these all count as the FIRST double crochet). Crochet 2 double crochets in the ring, crochet 2 chains. * Crochet 3 double crochets in the ring, crochet 2 chains. * Repeat * * another 2 x. Close with a slip stitch in the 3rd chain of the 1st double crochet. Now, turn your work!

Row 2: You will now crochet in the corner (the space between 2 chains). Crochet 3 chains,

Petra's square

Miriam's square

2 double crochets, 2 chains. In the same space, crochet 3 double crochets. Skip 3 double crochets and, in the next corner, crochet 3 double crochets, 2 chains, 3 double crochets. Skip 3 double crochets and, in the corner, crochet 3 double crochets, 2 chains, 3 double crochets. Skip 3 double crochets and, in the corner, crochet 3 double crochets, 2 chains, 3 double crochets. Close with a slip stitch in the 3rd chain of the first double crochet. Turn your work.

Row 3: Crochet 3 chains, 2 double crochets in the space between the 3 double crochet groups. Skip 3 double crochets and, in the corner, crochet 3 double crochets, 2 chains, 3 double crochets. Skip 3 double crochets and, in the corner, crochet 3 double crochets. Skip 3 double crochets and, in the corner, crochet 3 double crochets, 2 chains, 3 double crochets. Skip 3 double crochets and, in the corner, crochet 3 double crochets. Skip 3 double crochets and, in the corner, crochet 3 double crochets, 2 chains, 3 double crochets. Skip 3 double crochets and, in the corner, crochet 3 double crochets. Skip 3 double crochets and, in the corner, crochet 3 double crochets, 2 chains, 3 double crochets. Close with a slip stitch in the 3rd chain of the first double crochet. Turn your work.

Row 4: Crochet 3 chains, crochet 2 double crochets. Skip 3 double crochets and crochet 3 double crochets. Skip 3 double crochets and, in the corner, crochet 3 double crochets, 2 chains, 3 double crochets. Skip 3 double crochets and, in the corner, crochet 3 double crochets. Repeat another 1 x. Skip 3 double crochets and, in the corner, crochet 3 double crochets, 2 chains, 3 double crochets. Skip 3 double crochets and, in the corner, crochet 3 double crochets. Repeat another 1 x. Skip 3 double crochets and, in the corner, crochet 3 double crochets, 2 chains, 3 double crochets. Skip 3 double crochets and, in the corner, crochet 3 double crochets. Repeat another 1 x. Skip 3 double crochets and, in the corner, crochet 3 double crochets, 2 chains, 3 double crochets. Close with a slip stitch in the 3rd chain of the first double crochet.

Row 5: Crochet 3 chains, crochet 2 double crochets. Skip 3 double crochets and, in the corner, crochet 3 double crochets, 2 chains, 3 double crochets. Skip 3 double crochets and, in the corner, crochet 3 double crochets. Repeat another 2 x. Skip 3 double crochets and, in the corner, crochet 3 double crochets, 2 chains, 3 double crochets. Skip 3 double crochets and, in the corner, crochet 3 double crochets. Repeat another 2 x. Skip 3 double crochets and, in the corner, crochet 3 double crochets, 2 chains, 3 double crochets. Skip 3 double crochets and, in the corner, crochet 3 double crochets. Repeat another 2 x. Skip 3

double crochets and, in the corner, crochet 3 double crochets, 2 chains, 3 double crochets. Close with a slip stitch in the 3rd chain of the first double crochet.

Row 6 (crochet this row with the joining color): Crochet 3 chains (=1st double crochet), in every stitch, crochet 1 double crochet, in the corners, crochet 2 double crochets, 2 chains, 2 double crochets. Repeat this all the way around. Close the row with a slip stitch in the 3rd chain. Finish all loose yarn.

BREGJE'S PUFF-STITCH GRANNY SQUARE

A puff stitch is a group of stitches that look a little like bobbles or popcorn, but then just a little bit different. You make the stitch by crocheting a number of incomplete half double crochets that are only crocheted together at the very end.

INSTRUCTIONS FOR THE PUFF STITCH
Yarn over once, insert the crochet hook in the chain space, yarn over again, and pull the loop so that there are 3 loops on the hook. Make another yarn over and pull the loop so that there are 5 loops on the hook. Repeat this twice more so that there are 9 loops on the hook. Make a yarn over and pull the yarn through the first 8 loops. Yarn over again and pull the yarn through the last two loops. Your puff stitch is done.

Row 1: In a magic ring:
3 chains (counts as 1st double crochet), then 11 additional double crochets with 1 chain in between each. Close with a slip stitch in the 3rd chain of the row (= 12 double crochets). Crochet a slip stitch in the chain space to get in between the double crochets.

Row 2: 2 chains (counts as 1st half double crochet of the 1st puff stitch), crochet the 1st puff stitch according to the instructions above. Then, crochet 2 chains. Crochet 1 puff stitch and 2 chains in every chain space between the double crochets. Close with a slip stitch in the uppermost stitch of the 1st puff stitch. Crochet a slip stitch in the chain space to get above the space (= 12 puff stitches).

Row 3: 2 chains (counts as the 1st half double crochet of the 1st puff stitch). *Crochet 2 puff stitches and 2 chains in the next space between the puff stitches*. Repeat * * until the end of the row.

Bregje's square

Close with a slip stitch in the uppermost stitch of the 1st puff stitch. Crochet a slip stitch in the chain space to get above the space (= 24 puff stitches).

Row 4: 3 chains (counts as 1st double crochet) and another double crochet in the same space between the puff stitches. 2 half double crochets in the next space between the puff stitches.

2 single crochets in the next space between the puff stitches.

2 half double crochets in the next space between the puff stitches.

2 double crochets in the next space between the puff stitches.

Corner: In the next space between the puff stitches, crochet 2 triple crochets, 2 chains, 2 triple crochets.

In the next space: *2 double crochets, 2 half double crochets, 2 single crochets, 2 half double crochets and 2 double crochets.

In the next corner, again crochet 2 triple crochets, 2 chains, 2 triple crochets in the same space. * Repeat * * until the end of the row.

Your circle should now be a nice square.

Close the row with a slip stitch in the 3rd chain from the beginning of the row.

Row 5: 3 chains (counts as 1st double crochet). Crochet a double crochet in every stitch. In the space in the corners, crochet 2 double crochets, 2 chains, 2 double crochets.

Close with a slip stitch in the 3rd chain from the beginning of the row.

Row 6: Repeat row 5.

Row 7: Repeat row 5 in the joining color.

LIDY'S GRANNY SQUARE

Row 1: Make a magic ring, crochet 3 chains (= 1st double crochet), crochet 15 double crochets, 16 double crochets in total. Tighten with a slip stitch in the 3rd chain of the 1st double crochet.

Row 2: *Crochet 4 chains, skip 1 stitch, tighten with a slip stitch in the next stitch *. Repeat 7 times, 8 rounds in total. Close with a slip stitch in the first stitch of the first round.

Row 3: Crochet 1 slip stitch in the next round. Crochet 3 chains (= 1st double crochet), 2 double crochets, 2 chains, 3 double crochets in this same round, 1 chain, 1 single crochet in the next round, 1 chain. *Crochet 3 double crochets, 2 chains, 3 double crochets in the next round, 1 chain, 1 single crochet in the next round, 1 chain*, * * repeat another 2 x. Close with a slip stitch in the 3rd chain of the 1st double crochet.

Row 4: Crochet 3 half double crochets in the stitches until the corner. 3 chains (= 1st double crochet), 2 double crochets, 2 chains, 3 double crochets, 2 chains, 1 double crochet in the next space. Crochet 1 chain, 1 double crochet, 1 double crochet in the next space, 2 chains. * At the corner, 3 double crochets, 2 chains, 3 double crochets, crochet 2 chains, 1 double crochet in the next space, 1 chain, 1 double crochet in the next space, 2 chains *, Repeat * * another 2 x. Close with a slip stitch in the 3rd chain of the 1st double crochet.

Row 5: Crochet 3 half double crochets on each stitch until the corner, crochet 3 chains (= 1st double crochet), 2 double crochets, 2 chains, 3 double crochets. * Crochet 1 chain, 3 double crochets in the next space, 1 chain, skip 1 space, 3 double crochets in the next space, 1 chain, at the corner, 3 double crochets, 2 chains, 3 double crochets. * Repeat * * 3 x. Close with a slip stitch in the 3rd chain of the 1st double crochet.

Row 6: Crochet 3 chains (= 1st double crochet), 2 x 1 double crochet on every double crochet. * At the corner, 2 double crochets, 2 chains, 2 double crochets, 3 x 1 double crochet on every double crochet, 1 double crochet in the next space, 3 x 1 double crochet on every double crochet, 1 double crochet in the next space, 3 x 1 double crochet on every double crochet. * Repeat * * another 3 x. Close with a slip stitch in the 3rd chain of the 1st double crochet.

Row 7: Crochet this row in the joining color!

Crochet 3 chains (= 1st double crochet), crochet a double crochet on every double crochet, *crochet 2 double crochets on the corner, 2 chains, 2 double crochets, crochet a double crochet on every double crochet* Repeat * *. Close with a slip stitch in the 3rd chain of the 1st double crochet.

Lidy's square

PUTTING THE BLANKET TOGETHER

Lay all the granny squares on the ground in a large 8 x 8 square. Move the squares around until you are happy with the distribution of colors and patterns.

Crochet all the squares in rows of 8 x 8 squares together using single crochets. Use the joining color to do this. Crochet all the horizontal seams first and then the vertical seams. Finally, crochet two rows of double crochets on all of the edges. On the corners, crochet 2 double crochets, 3 chains, 2 double crochets.

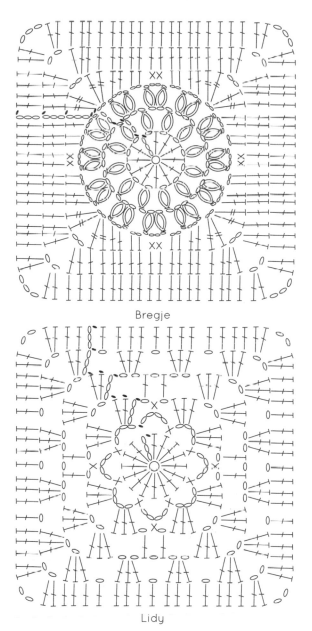

Bregje

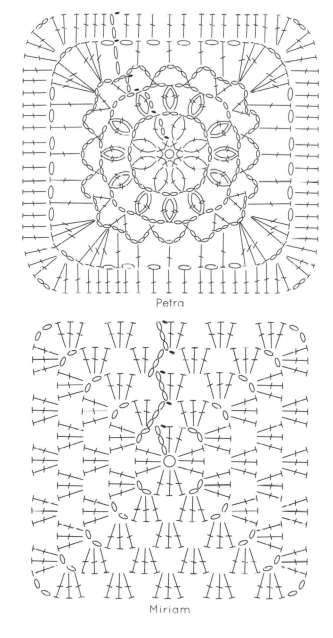

Petra

Lidy

The grey joining color is not shown in these drawings.

Miriam

• slip stitch	T half double crochet	bobble from 2 double crochets
◯ chain stitch		
X single crochet	double crochet	bobble from 4 double crochets
X single crochet in the back loop		
X single crochet in the previous row	triple crochet	puff stitch

GREEN YARN

1. LIDY'S TUNISIAN CROCHET CUSHION

SUPPLIES
Durable Cosy Fine, 3 balls, Mint (2137)
Tunisian crochet hook with long thread, number 8
Waffle fabric, 17.75 x 39.5 inches (45 x 100 cm)
Pins
Darning needle
Inner cushion, 15.75 x 15.75 inches (40 x 40 cm)

Tunisian crochet resembles crochet, but it's a little bit different. With Tunisian crochet, you need a long crochet hook or a crochet hook with a long thread and you keep all the stitches on your hook, which you then cast off all at once, with the exception of a single remaining stitch. **Important:** crochet loosely!

Personally, I don't measure everything out precisely to yield a 15.75 x 15.75 inch (40 x 40 cm) cushion. I usually just make a piece of crochet work that then becomes the size of the cushion. I make the inner cushion myself with two pieces of fabric and cushion filling, that way I can make whatever size cushion my crochet work yields.

If you do want the cushion to be 15.75 x 15.75 inches (40 x 40 cm), adjust your hook thickness and number of stitches accordingly. Make sure you always have an even number of stitches.

METHOD
With Tunisian crochet, the forward and return movements of the hook are treated as 1 row. You take all of the loops on to the forward pass and cast them off in the return pass.

TUNISIAN TULLE STITCH
Crochet 2 stitches together, make a loop by picking up the yarn from underneath 2 vertical stitches at once, and then make a loop by picking up the yarn through the 1st, foremost horizontal loop.

Make sure that you don't forget the last stitch—the edge stitch. Count the stitches on the needle regularly and pull your work straight so that you can clearly see your stitches. You need an even number of stitches to make this pattern.

TIP
If you take a break and put your work aside for a minute, be sure to write down which row you left off on.

Crochet a chain of 52 chain stitches.

Row 1: The loop on the hook is the 1st loop; take a loop through each of the stitches in the chain. You now have 52 loops on your hook. On the reverse pass, yarn over and pull it through 1 stitch and then yarn over and keep pulling it through 2 stitches until you are left with only one loop on your hook.

Row 2: The loop on your hook is the 1st stitch. * Crochet 2 stitches together, take up a loop by picking up the yarn under 2 vertical stitches at once, and then make a loop by picking up the yarn through the 1st, foremost horizontal loop. * Repeat. * * End with crocheting 2 together, 1 horizontal stitch and the edge stitch. There are now 52 stitches on the hook.
On the reverse pass, yarn over and pull it through 1 stitch and then yarn over and keep pulling it through 2 stitches until you are left with only one loop on your hook.

Row 3: The loop on your hook is the 1st stitch. Take up a loop through 1 vertical stitch, * take up a loop by picking up the yarn under 2 vertical stitches at once, and then make a loop by picking up the yarn through the 1st, foremost horizontal loop. * Repeat. * * End with 1 vertical stitch and the edge stitch. Repeat **rows 2 and 3** until your work is 15.75 inches (40 cm) long or achieves the desired length.

FINISHING (The stitches are on the hook as they were in row 2.) * Take up a loop through 2 vertical stitches and crochet a single crochet; take up a loop by stitching through the next space. Crochet a single crochet, * Repeat * * and finish. Finish all loose yarn.

SEWING THE COVER Cut two pieces, 16.25 x 16.25 inches (41 x 41 cm) each, of fabric. Lay the reverse side of your crochet work on to the good side of the fabric and sew it in place, all the way around. Pin the front and back to each other.

The stitched side faces up. Sew the two sides together and reinforce by sewing over the seam again. Iron the seams open. Rip open a bit of the stitching, stuff the cushion with filling, and sew the opening closed again, by hand.

2. PETRA'S CUSHION— HONEYCOMB KNIT

SUPPLIES
Durable Cosy Fine, 4 balls, Mint (2137)
Knitting needles, 10 (6 mm)
Waffle fabric, 39.5 x 14.5 inches (100 x 37 cm)
Pins
Darning needle
Inner cushion, 19.75 x 19.75 inches (50 x 50 cm)

Cast on 65 stitches (this pattern should be knit in 10 x 6 stitches + 5).

Row 1: wrong side: Knit 1, * slip 3 stiches purlwise (keep the yarn on the back), knit 3. * Repeat * * until the last 4 stitches; then, slip 3 stitches purlwise and knit 1.
Row 2: right side: Purl 1, * slip 3 stiches purlwise (keep the yarn on the front), purl 3. * Repeat * * until the last 4 stitches; then, slip 3 stitches purlwise and purl 1.
Row 3: Purl.
Row 4: Knit.
Row 5: Purl.
Row 6: Knit 2, * knit 1 together with the two loose yarns from rows 1 and 2 (insert the needle from the underside to the front under the two loose threads and knit the next stitch), knit 5 *. Repeat * * until

the last 3 stitches; then, knit 1 together with the two loose yarns from rows 1 and 2, knit 2.
Row 7: Knit 4, * slip 3 stiches purlwise (keep the yarn on the back), knit 3. * Repeat * * until the last stitch, knit 1.
Row 8: Purl 4, * slip 3 stiches purlwise (keep the yarn on the front), purl 3, * Repeat * * until the last stitch, purl 1.
Row 9: Purl.
Row 10: Knit.
Row 11: Purl.
Row 12: Knit 5, *knit 1 together with the two loose threads from rows 7 and 8, knit 5. * Repeat * * until the end.
Repeat rows 1 up to and including 12 another 10 x; finish with knit stitches in the next row.

SEWING THE BACK Cut two pieces of waffle fabric to size (14.5 x 19.75 inches [37 x 50 cm]). Fold 0.5 inch (1 cm) and then 1.25 inch (3 cm) on the wide side for the fold; stitch this along the edge, for both parts. Lay the good sides on top of each other so that you have a 19.75 x 19.75 inch (50 x 50 cm) square.

Pin the pieces in place on the sides and lay (good side to good side) your knit work on top of the fabric. Sew the cover along the edge, turn over the fold, and insert the inner cushion (19.75 x 19.75 inches [50 x 50 cm]).

3. BREGJE'S CABLE-KNIT CUSHION

SUPPLIES (for a cushion with one knit side)
Durable Cosy Fine, 4 balls, Mint (2137)
Knitting needles, 8 (5 mm)
Fabric for cushion cover, 20.5 x 40.25 inches (52 x 102 cm)
Pins
Darning needle
Inner cushion, 19.75 x 19.75 inches (50 x 50 cm)

GAUGE
14 stitches and 20 rows yields 4 x 4 inches (10 x 10 cm) in stocking stitch knit with size 8 (5 mm) needles. You may want to choose a needle that is a half size smaller or bigger. The knit work should feel robust.

Cast on 88 stitches (multiples of 6 plus 4 stitches).

Start right away with the counting pattern shown in the chart below. This chart shows the good side of your work. You always read the right rows (the uneven rows) from right to left.

Knit the first 8 stitches in accordance with the chart and then knit the repeat 6 times (this is the pattern repeated); knit the last 8 stitches according to the pattern. Knit all the rows in accordance with the vertical repeat and repeat this until the work is the desired length.

Loosely bind off all the stitches.

Fold the fabric for the cover in half with the good sides facing each other. Sew all the way around with a 0.5 inch (1 cm) seam, keeping an opening that is big enough to turn it inside out and to get the inner cushion inside.

Turn the piece of fabric right-side out and insert the inner cushion. Sew the opening closed with small, invisible stitches. Pin and stretch the knit work on to one side of the cushion and sew it in place, by hand.

Chart

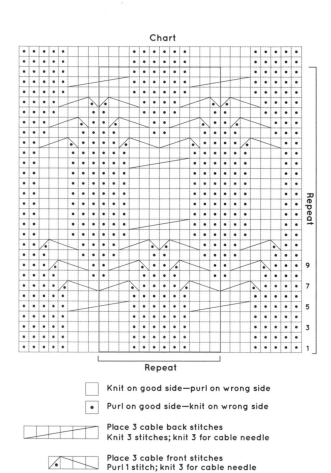

Repeat

Repeat

☐ Knit on good side—purl on wrong side

• Purl on good side—knit on wrong side

Place 3 cable back stitches
Knit 3 stitches; knit 3 for cable needle

Place 3 cable front stitches
Purl 1 stitch; knit 3 for cable needle

Place 1 cable back stitch
Knit 3 stitches; purl 1 for cable needle

4. MIRIAM'S ROUND CROCHET CUSHION
See drawing on page 136

SUPPLIES
Durable Cosy Fine, 3 balls, Mint (2137)
Crochet hook, J-10 (6 mm)
Darning needle
Fabric for cover, 23.75 x 23.75 inches (60 x 60 cm)
Pins
Darning needle or sewing machine
Cushion filling, about 19.75 inches (50 cm) diameter

When you are crocheting this round cushion, don't be worried if your work starts to get a little lumpy. This will disappear on its own after you finish a few more rows.

Make a magic ring of crochet 4 chains and close with a slip stitch. If you hook the starting thread into you work, you can tighten it later, which will give your ring of chains a nice, tight knit!

Row 1: Crochet 2 chains (= 1st double crochet), 1 double crochet, 1 chain in the ring, * crochet 2 double crochets together (= cluster), and 1 chain. * Repeat * *. Close with a slip stitch above the 1st cluster (7 clusters in total).
Row 2: Stitch through with 2 x a slip stitch on the chains in the previous row. Crochet 3 chains (= 1st double crochet) and 1 double crochet and 2 chains. * Crochet 2 double crochets and 2 chains on the chains in the previous row. * Repeat * *. Close with a slip stitch (7 groups in total).
Row 3: Stitch through with 2 x a slip stitch on the 2 chains in the previous row. Crochet 4 chains (= 1st double crochet) and 4 triple crochets. * Crochet 5 triple crochets on the 2 chains in the previous row. * Repeat * *. Close the row with a slip stitch (7 groups in total).
Row 4: Crochet 3 chains (= 1st double crochet). * In the next 3 stitches, crochet 1 double crochet; in the next stitch, crochet 2 double crochets. * In the next 4 stitches, crochet 1 double crochet; in the next stitch, crochet 2 double crochets * Repeat * *. Close with a slip stitch in the 3rd chain.
Row 5: Crochet 3 chains (= 1st double crochet). * In the next 4 stitches, crochet 1 double crochet; in the next stitch, crochet 2 double crochets. * In the next 5 stitches, crochet 1 double crochet; in the next stitch, crochet 2 double crochets * Repeat * *. Close with a slip stitch in the 3rd chain.

Row 6: * Crochet 6 chains (= 1st single crochet + 5 chains), skip 3 stitches, and in the next stitch, crochet 1 single crochet. * Crochet 5 chains, skip 3 stitches, and in the next stitch, crochet 1 single crochet. * Repeat * *. Close with a slip stitch in the 1st chain.

Row 7: Crochet 1 chain (= 1st single crochet). * Crochet 9 double crochets around the chain round and 1 single crochet on the single crochet. * Repeat * *. Close with a slip stitch in the 1st chain.

Row 8: Crochet 5 chains (= 1st single crochet + 4 chains), 4 chains, and 1 single crochet on the 5th double crochet. Crochet 4 chains and 1 single crochet on the single crochet. * Crochet 1 single crochet, 4 chains, 1 single crochet on the 5th double crochet, 4 chains, and 1 single crochet * Repeat * *. Close with a slip stitch in the 1st chain.

Row 9: Crochet 1 chain. * Crochet 5 half double crochets around the chain round. * Repeat * *. Close with a slip stitch in the 1st chain.

Row 10: Crochet 1 chain (= 1st single crochet). * Crochet 1 single crochet in the back loop of every stitch. * Close with a slip stitch in the turning chain.

Row 11: Repeat row 10.

Row 12: Crochet 3 chains (= 1st double crochet). Crochet 1 double crochet in every stitch. Close with a slip stitch in the 3rd chain of the 1st double crochet.

Row 13: * Crochet 4 chains (= 1st single crochet + 3 chains), skip 2 stitches, and crochet 1 single crochet in the next stitch. * Crochet 3 chains, skip 2 stitches, and crochet 1 single crochet in the next stitch * Repeat * *. Close with a slip stitch in the 1st chain.

Row 14: Crochet 1 chain. * Crochet 5 single crochets around the chain round. * Repeat * *. Close with a slip stitch in the 1st chain.

Row 15: Crochet 1 chain. * Crochet 1 single crochet on the next 4 stitches in the back loop. Then, crochet 1 deep—long—single crochet on the single crochet in row 13. * Repeat * *. Close with a slip stitch in the 1st chain.

Row 16: Crochet 3 chains (= 1st double crochet); crochet 1 double crochet in every stitch except for the "long single crochet," you skip that one. * Repeat * *. Close with a slip stitch in the 3rd chain of the 1st double crochet.

Row 17: Crochet 1 chain (= 1st single crochet); crochet a single crochet in every stitch. Close with a slip stitch.

Row 18: Crochet 2 chains (= 1st half double crochet), crochet a half double crochet in every stitch, and close with a slip stitch.

Row 19: Crochet 1 chain (= 1st single crochet); crochet 1 single crochet in the back loop of every stitch. Close with a slip stitch.

SEWING THE CUSHION Cut out the fabric double, with a diameter of 20.5 inches (52 cm). Lay your crochet work on the good side of (one piece of) the fabric and carefully pin it in place. I sewed my cushions on the sewing machine. If you position your machine foot right between the two ribs in the last rows, you should be able to sew your crochet work neatly on to the fabric.

Lay the two circles on top of each other with the good sides facing inward and pin them in place, leaving a small opening that will allow you to turn the cover right-side out and fill the cushion. Sew the pieces together. You can also sew in a nice label sticking out of the seam. Turn the cover right-side out, fill the cushion, and sew the opening closed, by hand.

MIRIAM'S RIBBON XL RUG

SUPPLIES

Hoooked Ribbon XL, 7 spools, color: Emerald
Crochet hook, N/P-15 (10 mm)
Large darning needle

You start the rug exactly as you did the round cushion. Crochet up to and including row 18 and continue as follows:

Row 19: Crochet 1 chain; crochet 1 single crochet in the back loop of each stitch. Close with a slip stitch.

Row 20: Repeat row 19.

Row 21: Crochet 3 chains (= 1st double crochet). Crochet a single crochet in every stitch. Close with a slip stitch.

Row 22: Crochet 1 chain (= 1st single crochet). * Crochet 4 chains, skip 3 stitches, and crochet 1 single crochet in the next stitch. * Repeat * *. Close with a slip stitch.

The rug has a diameter of 43.25 inches (110 cm).

Row 23: Crochet 1 chain. * Crochet 7 double crochets around the chain round and crochet 1 single crochet in the single crochet. * Repeat * *. Close with a slip stitch.

Row 24: * Crochet 1 single crochet, 3 chains, 1 single crochet in the 4th double crochet, 3 chains. And 1 single crochet on the next single crochet. * Repeat * *. Close with a slip stitch.

Row 25: Crochet 1 chain. * Crochet 3 double crochets around the chain round. * Repeat * *. Close with a slip stitch.

Row 26: Crochet 1 chain (= 1st single crochet); crochet 1 single crochet in the back loop of every stitch. Close with a slip stitch.

Row 27: Crochet 2 chains (= 1st half double crochet); crochet 1 half double crochet in the back loop of every stitch. Close with a slip stitch.

Row 28: Crochet 3 chains, (= 1st single crochet); crochet 1 single crochet in the back loop of every stitch. Close with a slip stitch. Finish all loose threads.

TIP
This garland can also be made with other materials, like cotton yarn or glitter yarn to hang over your patio table.

MIRIAM'S JUTE GARDEN GARLAND

I like to hang garlands up with the garden, too! And how cool is this rustic, jute garland!

SUPPLIES
Hoooked Natural Jute, 2 spools, colors: Lush Petrol and Serenity Mint
Crochet hook, N/P-15 (10 mm)
Very large darning needle

I crocheted 3 granny squares from 1 spool of jute. Crochet 6 basic granny squares see page 128, Miriam's traditional granny square), but only crochet rows 1 and 2 and then finish the loose threads.

Cut a piece of jute that is about 98.5 inches (250 cm) long and baste the 6 granny squares on to it. Tie a loop into both ends and hang up your garland!

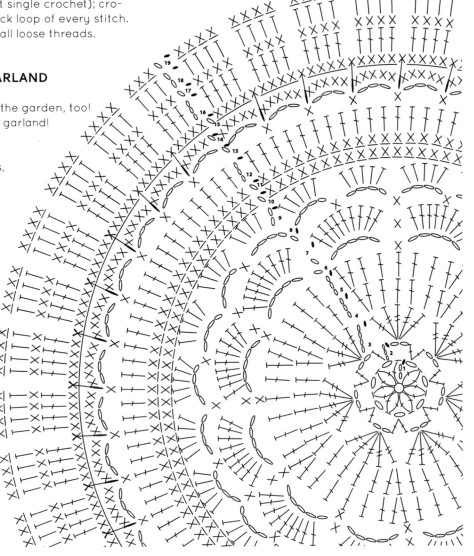

ITALIAN SCARVES

LIDY'S ITALIAN SCARF

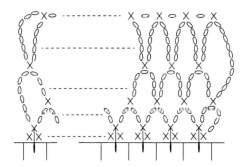

SUPPLIES

Linen fabric, 15.75 x 59 inches
  (40 x 150 cm)
Sewing machine
Borgo de'Pazzi Fresco, 1 ball,
  color 18 (Teal)
Crochet hook, E-4 (3.5 mm)
Embroidery needle with
  point
A larger crochet hook for the
  tassels
A ruler and a vanishing fabric
  marker (optional)

Crochet stitches used: single
crochets and chain stitches

METHOD

Cut the fabric to size, if necessary, along the bias so
  that you end up with a nice, straight piece of fabric.
Hem the edges 0.75 x 0.5 inch (2 x 1 cm) folded over
  and stitch these in place on the sewing machine, 0.5
  inch (1 cm) wide.
Festoon the edge, all the way around, using a festoon
  stitch, with the Fresco, with each stitch spaced about
  0.5 inch (1 cm) apart. (Tip! Use a ruler and vanishing
  fabric marker to mark the distance.)

Now, you will crochet the edges. Attach the yarn and
  crochet 2 single crochets on each festoon stitch,
  starting on a long side. Crochet a chain on the corner.

Row 1: On the short side, crochet 2 single crochets on
  each festoon stitch.
Row 2: Crochet 6 chains; attach with a single crochet
  in the 1st round. * Crochet 4 chains; attach with a
  single crochet in the next round. * Repeat * * up to
  and including the last round. Turn your work.
Row 3: Crochet 9 chains; attach with a single crochet
  in the 1st round. * Crochet 7 chains; attach with a
  single crochet in the next round. * Repeat * * up to
  and including the last round. Turn your work.
Row 4: Crochet 15 chains; attach with a single crochet
  in the 1st round *. Crochet 10 chains; attach with a
  single crochet in the next round. * Repeat * * up to
  and including the last round. Turn your work.
Row 5: Crochet 7 chains; attach with a single crochet
  in the next round. * Crochet 1 chain; 1 single crochet
  in the next round. * Repeat * * up to and including
  the last round. Attach to the other long side of the
  scarf and repeat row 1. Crochet through row 1 on the
  short side and repeat rows 2 to 5 there. Finish all the
  loose threads.

TASSELS

Cut 11.75 inch (30 cm) pieces of yarn. I use a hairpin
lace loom, but you can also just wrap the yarn around
a piece of cardboard or a box, measuring how long
the distance around is.

Take 4 pieces, stick the crochet hook in the small
space on the underside, fold the yarn pieces double,
and pull them, using the hook, through your crochet
work, pulling the strands through the loop on your
hook. Make tassels on both undersides.

BREGJE'S ITALIAN SCARF

SUPPLIES

Piece of linen,
  19.75 x 47.25 inches
  (50 x 120 cm)
Washable felt pen
Borgo de'Pazzi Fresco,
  1 ball color 16 (Rose-
  wood) and 1 ball color
  28 (Think Pink)
Crochet hook B-1
  (2 or 2.5 mm)
Embroidery needle
  with a point
Pins (optional)
Water bottle (optional)

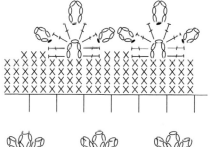

To make my scarf, I cut my piece of linen in two and sewed the short ends together. This made a long strip that was 9.75 x 94.5 inches (25 x 240 cm). I sewed a 0.5 inch (1 cm) French seam around all the edges.

Using a washable felt pen, I plotted out 0.5 inch (1 cm) dots all the way around the outside of the scarf. I used the dots to guide my festoon stitch. I used Fresco color 16 for the festooning.

CROCHET EDGE

Row 1: With the good side facing you, attach color 16 on the right-hand side of one of the long edges. Crochet 3 single crochets in each festoon stitch. On the short ends, make sure that you have a multiple of 9 plus 7 extra stitches so that the crowns work out later.

Row 2: 1 single crochet in every single crochet. Close off.

Row 3: Attach color 28 on the right-hand side of a long edge.

* (1 single crochet, 4 chains, 1 slip stitch) in the 1st single crochet; (1 single crochet, 5 chains, 1 slip stitch) in the next single crochet; (1 single crochet, 4 chains, 1 slip stitch) in the next single crochet; 1 single crochet in each of the next 5 single crochets. * Repeat * * until the end of the row; you end the last 3 single crochets with a crown picot (you can cheat here a little to be able to end with a picot).

Crochet 1 chain on the corner and then a row of single crochets on the short side, 1 chain on the corner. On the next long side, crochet another row of crown picots, as described above. 1 chain on the corner and crochet another row of single crochets along the short side. The long edges are done. The short sides are still due a bigger crown.

Do not close; crochet a chain to allow you to turn your work.

Row 4: You are now working on the "wrong" side of your work.

In each of the first 3 single crochets, crochet 1 single crochet; * 5 chains; in each of the next 9 single crochets 1 single crochet; * Repeat * *; finish with 4 single crochets. Crochet a chain and turn your work.

Row 5: You are now working on the good side of your work again.

Now, crochet your large crown in the chain loops in the previous row;

* 2 double crochets, 5 chains, 1 slip stitch in the first of these chains, 2 double crochets, 6 chains, 1 slip stitch in the first of these chains, 2 double crochets, 5 chains, 1 slip stitch in the first of these chains, 2 double crochets; skip 2 single crochets and crochet 1 single crochet in each of the next 3 single crochets. * Repeat * * until the end of the row. You will end with a large crown. Close the row with a slip stitch in the first single crochet of the previous row. Finish the loose threads.

Attach color 28 to the good side of the right-hand side of the other short side. Rows 4 and 5, as described above.

Finish all the loose threads and block your scarf, if you'd like, by pinning it to a soft surface and spraying it with water in a spray bottle until damp.

MIRIAM'S ITALIAN SCARF

SUPPLIES

A piece of linen, 19.75 x 55 inches (50 x 140 cm)
Borgo de'Pazzi Hannah, color Grey 22
Borgo de'Pazzi Fresco, color Natural 10
Borgo de'Pazzi Fresco, color Mint 12
Crochet hook D (3mm)
Vanishing fabric marker
Sharp needle
Clover Tassel Maker Small

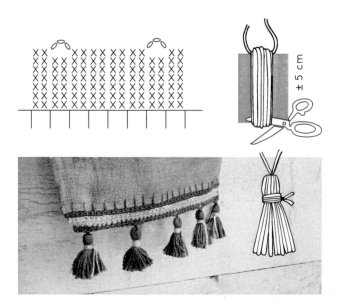

Fold the fabric in half, widthwise (= 9.75 x 55 inches [25 x 140 cm]) and sew the long side closed with a 0.75 inch (2 cm) seam. Turn the scarf over. Fold both ends 0.5 inch (1 cm) inward, iron them flat, if necessary, and neatly stitch them closed.

You will crochet along both short ends of your scarf. Plot out dots, 0.5 inch (1 cm) apart, using a vanishing fabric marker about 0.5 inch (1 cm) above the edge. Use these dots to apply your festoon stich using the Hannah (9 inches [23 cm] in width = 23 festoon stitches).

CROCHET EDGE

Row 1: Using the Hannah Grey, crochet 1 single crochet in the first vertical festoon stitch and then crochet 2 single crochets in each horizontal festoon stitch. At the end of the row, 1 single crochet in the last vertical festoon stitch = 48 single crochets.

Row 2: Crochet 1 turning chain; crochet 1 single crochet in every stitch.

Row 3: Using Fresco Natural, crochet 1 turning chain and then 1 single crochet in every stitch.

Rows 4 and 5: Using Fresco Mint, crochet 1 turning chain and then 1 single crochet in every stitch.

Row 6: Using Hannah Grey, crochet 1 turning chain and then 1 single crochet in every stitch.

Row 7: Crochet 1 turning chain and then, in the next 2 stitches, 1 single crochet, crochet 3 chains, skip 2 stitches. In the next 8 stitches, crochet 1 single crochet. Repeat 4x. In the last 3 stitches, crochet 1 single crochet.

TASSELS

Using the Clover Tassel Maker, make 10 tassels using the Hannah Grey. Use the smallest size (you can also just use a sturdy piece of cardboard, 3.25 x 3.5 inches [8.5 x 9 cm]) and wrap the yarn around it about 15 to 20 times. Then, wrap a piece of Hannah Grey around the middle (underneath the yarn on the spool).

Tie it tightly around the other strands and then cut through the wrapped threads on the top and the bottom. Fold the bouquet of yarn in half and bind it together using 2 strands of Fresco yarn. Tie the tassels to the crochet loops along the edge. Carefully finish any remaining loose threads.

PETRA'S ITALIAN SCARF

SUPPLIES

Piece of linen, 19.75 x 59 inches [50 x 150 cm], Arella color 106
Tapestry needle
Crochet hook B-1 (2.5 mm)
Sewing machine

Cut the fabric lengthwise, through the middle. You will have two pieces that are 9.75 x 59 inches (25 x 150 cm) each. Sew these to each other diagonally; lay the two pieces of fabric in such a way that the ends are perpendicular to one another and stitch a 45-degree seam from one corner to the other. Cut a 0.5 inch (1.5 cm) seam, cut a half off at 0.25 inch (5 mm), and finish as a flat seam.

You can now cut your scarf to the desired length, 78.75 inches (200 cm), for example. Finish the outside edge with an ironed or sewn hem.

Festoon stitch the outside edges of the scarf using the off-white yarn (use the hem as a guide) and keep your stitches about 0.5 inch (1 cm) apart.

CROCHET EDGE

Attach the off-white yarn using the crochet hook and crochet trim of leaves all the way around. To do this, keep crocheting the following: * 3 single crochets in 1 festoon stitch, next festoon stitch: 1 single crochet, 5 chains, slip stitch in the single crochet, 4 chains and a slip stitch in the same single crochet, 1 single crochet. * Repeat * *.

CRAFT DATES—MATERIALS

Especially for you, and with our input, Eline designed a variety of materials that will help you to personalize or add to your Craft Date or handiwork project. Punch your own hanging labels out of beautiful pastel design paper, for example, and stamp a fun, appropriate image and text on to it.

You can do this kind of punching using **Craft Dates** die cutting templates. These are metal templates that you can use to punch paper, cardstock, fabric, felt, metal foil, or thin (faux) leather. You'll need a punch machine to do this, such as the Big Shot from Sizzix. Our Craft Date die cutting template set's article number is COL1445 and includes templates for, among other things, a beautiful Japanese pair of scissors, a few labels, and a spool (that you can even wrap real thread around).

The **Craft Dates design paper** comes in nice, pastel colors and features geometric patterns. The paper comes in an A5 size pad. There are eight patterns included of which there are four sheets of each. The article number of the paper is PB7054.

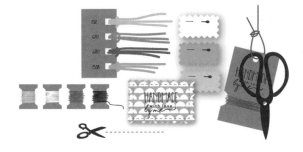

Then, there are the **Craft Date stamps**, also known as clear stamps, which are transparent, rubber-like stamps that you mount on to specially-designed Plexiglas blocks (acrylic) before you stamp. The back of the stamp automatically adheres to the smooth surface of the Plexiglas, and this combination functions together as your stamp.

The great part is, these stamps allow you to see through them so you can see exactly where your stamped image will appear. Use good stamp ink and don't press the stamp into the stamp pad. Place your stamp, stamp-side up, beside the ink pad and then dab the ink pad on to the stamp.

StazOn ink is a good option as it allows you to stamp on to just about anything—including smooth surfaces and even fabric! You can even (carefully) wash the stamped fabric, which makes it great fun to stamp your own fabric labels.

Do watch out for stains though, once this ink gets on to something, it never comes off . . . Clean your stamps and Plexiglas block after use with lukewarm water and a mild soap.

There are two Craft Date stamp sets—both of which include stamps with craft-related texts and images. Combine the texts with the images to your heart's desire. The article numbers of these sets are EC0166 and EC0167.

The die cutting templates (called Collectables), as well as the stamps and the paper, are produced by Marianne Design (www.mariannedesign.nl) and are available for purchase at www.craftdates.nl and in hobby (web) shops that sell paper and stamps.

OUR FAVORITES

MAGAZINES
vtwonen
Ariadne at Home
KOEL Magazine
Boligliv (Denmark)
Living & More (Germany)
Mollie Makes (UK)
Simply Living (UK)
amirisu (Japan)

CRAFT BOOKS
Simple Colour Knitting (Erika Knight)
Breien voor Starters [Knitting for Beginners] (Erika Knight)
Scandinavian Gatherings (Melissa Bahen)
How to Style your Brand (Fiona Humberstone)
De Bijbel van het Breiwerk [The Knitting Bible] (Marie Claire/Phildar)
Knitting Block by Block (Nicky Epstein)
Merchant & Mills Sewing Book (Carolyn N. K. Denham)
HOME (Vtwonen)

STORES (CRAFTS)

United States
A.C. Moore www.acmoore.com
Daniel Smith www.danielsmith.com
Dharma Trading Company
 www.dharmatrading.com
Dick Blick www.dickblick.com
Hobby Lobby www.hobbylobby.com
Joann Fabrics and Crafts www.joann.com
Michael's www.michaels.com
Purl Soho (New York) www.purlsoho.com
Target www.target.com
Wal-Mart www.walmart.com

Europe
Meet & Make (Leiden) www.meetmake.nl
Rits In (Zwolle) www.ritsin.nl
Echtstudio (Alphen aan den Rijn)
 www.echtstudio.nl
Juffrouw Lanterfant (Groningen)
 www.juffrouwlanterfant.nl
Cross & Woods (The Hague)
 www.crossandwoods.com
Wolplein (Zaltbommel) www.wolplein.nl
Van der Lee Stoffen (Hilversum)
 www.vdleestoffen.nl
Julija's Shop (Antwerp) www.julijasshop.be
Loop London (London)
 www.loopknittingshop.com

Frieda Hain (Berlin) www.friedahain.de
Merchant & Mills (Rye, East Sussex)
 www.merchantandmills.com

Asia
Check & Stripe (Tokyo) www.checkandstripe.com

Online
Fringe Supply Co. (online store)
 www.fringesupplyco.com
Bedijs (online store) www.bedijs.nl

STORES (OTHER)
Pluum Lekkers & Leuks (Bussum and Leiden,
 home accessories) www.pluumwinkel.nl
't Haagje (Huizen, also online store, home accessories, clothing, gifts) www.thaagje.nl
Petit Pan (Paris, also online store, fabrics and
 miscellaneous) www.petitpan.com
Hella Duijs (online store, ceramics)
 www.helladuijs.nl
Deens.nl (online store, home accessories)
 www.deens.nl
Ompak (online store, paper and stationary)
 www.ompak.nl
Søstrene Grene (stores throughout the Nether-
 lands, miscellaneous and crafts)
 www.sostrenegrene.com/nl

SPONSORS

We want to thank our sponsors so much for their enthusiasm, trust in us, and for the beautiful materials that we got to work with in the making of this book.

G. Brouwer & Zn
Thank you, Remco and Gerrit Brouwer and your team for the most beautiful colors of Durable yarn, fabrics, paint, and the vast quantities of haberdashery (www.gbrouwer.nl).

Marianne Design
Thank you, Marianne Perlot for the production of our very own Craft Dates stamps, paper, and die cutting templates (www.mariannedesign.nl).

Borgo De'Pazzi
Thank you, Bert Noorderijk, Carlo Signori and Masimo Signori for the amazing yarn from Borgo de'Pazzi (www.bnagenturen.nl).

Stik 'n Stof
Thank you, Marlies Lammers for the wonderful linen and oilskin fabrics and, our favorite, Merchant & Mills haberdashery (www.stikenstof.nl).

Hoooked
Thank you, Anouk Milani for the lovely Natural Jute and Ribbon XL yarn (www.hoooked.nl).

THANKS

Thanks to Anna Visser from Lait Fotografie for the beautiful photography.

Thanks to Antoinette van Schaik from A vormgeving & dtp for making this book ready for print.

Thanks to Miriam Catshoek for the use of her house and garden as locations for photoshoots.

Thanks to Marike den Brok from Publisher Luiting-Sijthoff for her faith in our concept.

Thanks to Linda van Loon from Buitengewoon Lekker in Almere for the use of this beautiful location for the "Secret Craft Date" we held for our testers.

A big thank you to our pattern testers: Lotte (lottehaakt), Sanne (sosanne85), Ingrid (ingrid68), Marianne (marretjeroos), Anique (kleinmaarfijn_anique), Caroline (carolineseignette), Jacqueline (huisen-haak), Manon (petit_petite_nl), Evelien (rits_in_zwolle), Mieke (rits_in_zwolle), Minke (minkesthuis), Chantal (sjantietop), Ingrid (sunny_designs), Noortje (liefsvan-noor), Liset (tantosetje), Bernadet (made_byjet) and Marlies (stiknstof).